MOMLANDIA

MOMLANDIA

An Imperfect Guide to Organic Mothering

JENNIFER STRUBE

edited by Samantha Lemos

RESOURCE *Publications* · Eugene, Oregon

MOMLANDIA
An Imperfect Guide to Organic Mothering

Resource Publications
An Imprint of Wipf and Stock Publishers
199 W. 8th Ave., Suite 3
Eugene, OR 97401

www.wipfandstock.com

PAPERBACK ISBN:978-1-7252-9125-6
HARDCOVER ISBN: 978-1-7252-9124-9
EBOOK ISBN: 978-1-7252-9126-3

02/09/21

To our amazing mothers,
Linda and Sheryl,
who paved the way to glory.
You both made it look so easy.
All our hearts forever.

-Jen and Sam

The moment a child is born,

the mother is also born.

She never existed before.

The woman existed, but the mother, never.

A mother is something absolutely new.

—BHAGWAN SHREE RAJNEESH

Contents

Baby Dreams

JANUARY 2018

I can't believe this, Sam. How in the world are we both pregnant at the same time?

Twenty years after college! Talk about timing.

And due three weeks apart?

Both with baby girls? It's truly a gift, Jen.

Our little ones will be best friends.

On opposite coasts.

And write letters.

And plan trips.

And know they have rad moms.

This is going to be the best adventure of our lives!

I can't wait.

◆◆◆◆◆

ONE YEAR LATER, JANUARY 2019, 2:15 A.M.

Are you up? Sorry I'm texting so late/early.

I quit! I've given her baby massage and rubbed lavender oils all over her angel-kissed body and sung her French lullabies and read her Neruda poetry and breastfed her by candlelight and this biotch still won't sleep!

Damn princesses need the Shangri-La.

If she gets the Shangri-La, where're our palaces?

Burned down with our former lives.

Oh right. Welcome to Momlandia.

Before Baby

SEPTEMBER 8, 2018

I am sprawled upon my couch with my feet propped high on pillows. My knees are posted outward, and my gaze is towards the sky. My cat purrs in approval, curled contently in my crotch, securely guarding the exit.

I am in a hypnobirthing class in my foyer, deep breathing my baby to life.

Our birth coach hovers beside us, guiding our birthing postures. "Dad, give her confidence. Trust her and remind her to breathe. Ask her what she needs and keep offering her food and water."

My cat remains posted at position, convinced this is all for her.

The coach hands me affirmation cards, as I announce peace to my womb.

My baby is in the right position.
My uterus is supple and soft.
I breathe my baby to freedom.

I repeat these phrases ad nauseum, humming along to the Aboriginal Flute playlist echoing in the background. When I finish my affirmations, I gaze at my loving husband, fully asleep on the couch. My darling husband, the father of our pending child, the man who succumbed to hypnosis. How dare he snooze through my uterine pep-talk! If he sleeps during the pretend birth, he's sure to doze off during go-time! I shove my elbow in his side and give him the dainty I-love-you-death-stare, while he defends his slumber; it was my fault for making the practice birth so mellow.

Assured of my deep love for him, I return to the task at hand: birth practice. The hypnobirthing coach turns us to face each other, my belly bump touching his dad-bod, and wraps my arms around his waist. This is the slow dance pose. She rocks us back and forth, our feet waddling like awkward middle school dance partners, until she announces, "Surge!" Then, I pretend-feel my contractions and drop it like it's J-Lo hot.

From the ground, I glow like a virile goddess.

I hover there, proud of my stoop, but there's only one problem with J-Lo. Nobody can get up from this squat. My darling husband hoists me up from up the floor, nearly breaking his back, while the coach gives us homework to practice until next week. She recommends rehearsing more labor positions and gives us a brochure of stick figure postures that make birthing easier. She also gives us a list of meditations to listen to and mantras to recite, as well as foods and gentle stretches to practice. I make a pre-labor workout schedule and tape it to our kitchen wall.

We will be birthing legends.

How did I get here? Well, as an approaching mother-to-be, I had only one pending goal: avoid the epidural at all costs.

Now I'd like to tell you it's because I am femme-au-naturel, because I use aluminum-free deodorant and paraben-free shampoo and because frankly there's only one way my baby is coming into the world, and that is with an organic sticker on her head. And while most of that is true, there was really one reason that topped my list.

I'm terrified of needles.

Truly, I faint when I see them. I'm the almost forty-year-old that asks for a baby butterfly pricker when she gets her blood drawn. And sitting up in those orange plastic chairs? Oh, heck no! I ask for the invalid room, the one with paper cushioned recliners and juice boxes. I stare at the wall, deep breathe, and hum Sunday School songs so I don't hear the sound of the rubber band snap around my veins while the nurse . . .

I'll stop there. It's just too traumatic to talk about.

So, as you see, my fear of needles sent me on a wild baby goose chase called "natural labor." Because in the 21st century, no American gives birth naturally without taking a ridiculous number of classes to learn what their bodies already know how to do.

This is not new. Women have always known that NATURAL takes work. Natural is not effortless. Natural is not "roll out of bed with sexy tousled hair." That's not a real thing. That look involves four hair products and a YouTube tutorial. Natural rarely happens naturally. I don't care how many farm-to-table meals you eat or how much you reduce-reuse-recycle. Even for the most granola of us, babies don't just naturally fall out of you. It doesn't matter if you saw that girl give birth in a taxi on the evening recap. That is #fakenews, friends.

Thus, in my search to learn the "natural" way, I signed up for every prenatal course I could: hypnobirthing, midwife circles, couples birthing class. They unanimously carried the overarching commandment—do ALL things to avoid induction. If you get induced, the contractions come closer and more intensely, and only the most badass of mothers can survive that pressure without the epidural. I am not a badass, so I took note.

How does one avoid induction? Apparently, it's simple and "natural." Starting at thirty-six weeks, all you have to do is:

1. *Have weekly acupuncture.*

2. *Make love four times a week and lay still afterward for a few hours, preferably days.*

3. *Eat six dates a day. Make sure it's six.*

4. *Top everything you eat with arugula.*

5. *Massage your boobs at every stoplight.*

6. *Reverse massage direction at intersections.*

7. *If you are one week late, drink three cups of penny oil tea.*

8. *If you are twelve days late, drink tea plus start breast pumping.*

9. *Drink castor oil on day thirteen and then eat ice cream. The two balance each other alchemically.*

10. *Pour warm almond oil on your vag to help it soften.*

11. *Talk to your baby and encourage her to come out. Tell her you are ready.*

12. *Drink juice thirty minutes before you get a non-stress test at the doctor, so your baby does the juice dance and the doctor doesn't stress you out.*

This is the organically simple formula to avoid a Texas-sized needle and to have a "natural" birth. Don't get me wrong—all infants are 100% organic and perfect, however they come out. There is no unnatural birth, nor unnatural baby, and to be honest, c-section babies have the cutest heads. But darn it, if I can avoid that freakishly large epidural, I won't faint during the birth of my child and a conscious mom is always a victory.

Let's do this.

Baby Time

SEPTEMBER 2

Meet Enora! She is 6 pounds, 12 ounces, and we are all healthy and strong.

Oh Sam, she's spectacular. I might be weeping in her honor.

It was a three-day labor. I'm pretty sure we prayed all 150 Psalms and used every existing rebozo technique to get her out.

You are my heroine. How are you? WHERE are you?

We just got home from the hospital. I have so much to share but am too tired to type. Just wanted you to know she's here.

She's miraculous.

Your bambino is coming soon!

Two weeks, fingers crossed. Get some rest.

◆◆◆◆◆

SEPTEMBER 15

Miracle cure alert! Be sure to have this on hand when you come home from the hospital: Earth Mama Organic Perineum Balm.

What's a perineum?

You'll find out soon, although you should technically be massaging it now for stretching purposes.

I thought all I had left to do was set up the nursery.

Oh, a whole new world awaits you . . . on a magic carpet ride.

I won't dare close my eyes.

Trust me, though, the cream heals everything down there. Sorry if this is TMI, but trust me and go buy it. Okay, baby's hungry. I can't wait until you jump into this with me! There's sooo much to share.

◆◆◆◆◆

Birth is a blur. By blur, I mean twenty-three hours of tribal warfare, where I beckon every ancestor from California to Antarctica while the angels escort my cherub into the world. And by angels, I mean my husband and doula, who feed me steak between yoga ball bounces and tub swirling and

13

downward dog and the intensely spiritual God-you-better-part-that-Red-Sea pose.

And then, voila! A darling, precious daughter—a miracle of transcendental imagination. Her tiny toes, her pink fingers, her whispy specks of hair, her blazing blue eyes. Every inch of her is perfection. I had made a human (with the help of God and the husband, of course). My saintly husband, who couldn't have been a better champion at my side, stood by me every step of the way with no needles in sight! Eureka! It is finished. The hard part is over. I clutch my baby to my chest and melt into motherhood the way an ice cream cone drips into summer—in complete rocky road bliss.

♦♦♦♦♦

MOTHERHOOD: DAY ONE

I'm lying in a hospital bed with giant gauze wrapped between my thighs and two suction cups clutching my breasts. I am only hours postpartum, and the lactation consultant has arrived to teach me how to pump.

"This will help your milk come in," she informs me, attaching two suction cups to my chest. The cups each have a long plastic tube that lead to a chambray-yellow vacuum, the kind you see in futuristic '70s sitcoms. "These are the setting knobs," she says, pointing to two dials on the pumping machine. "One is for suction and the other is for speed. You want to start both slowly and then work up to what's comfortable. I'll start at level one."

She turns the knobs and I hear a rumbling sound, but it doesn't sound like your typical household appliance. It sputters like a contraption from another planet, inhaling and exhaling mechanically like an out-of-breath Darth Vader. Suddenly, I realize I'm no longer on earth. I've been teleported to a very foreign land where my body is no longer mine.

And then I feel it—that warm, fuzzy feeling where a sci-fi machine rips my nipples off.

Sensing my horror, the nurse pats me on the shoulder and says, "You'll get used to it," as though I'm now a bovine clone in her outer space experiment. I stare at her and then back at this contraption. The suction cups are actually more like funnels you use for an oil change. The little funnel wraps around my lady parts, moving them back and forth mechanically until they grow as large as GMO products. Once enlarged, two baby bottles hang ready to collect my fluid, one life-sucking drop at a time. Meanwhile, the machine hums it's melodic alien song, swapping between low and high settings, tearing my precious parts off slowly one droplet at a time.

I've been abducted to Momlandia.

"You actually won't get milk today," the nurse says. "You'll get the even better stuff—colostrum. It's thicker, full of protein, fights infection, fortifies the GI tract, and is so packed with vitamins and minerals, it's the richest food your child will ever eat in her life." As she speaks, her voice becomes monotone and her eyes glaze over, as though she's beaming herself back to Boobland.

My husband touches my arm, returning my focus to the room. "See!" he says. "You are giving her the best food possible."

Yes, I remind myself. This is worth it. I am producing a Michelin-starred meal for my daughter, all for free, minus the $20,000 hospital bill that will hit our insurance next week. I can do this.

After ten minutes on the pump, the nurse turns off the machine and unscrews the bottles, showing me my magic. "You have an ounce on each side. Impressive," she says, placing the bottles on the armrest. "You can feed this to your daughter via a little syringe when she wakes."

"Can't I just breastfeed her?"

"Yes, but we don't want to waste this. It's liquid gold."

"Of course not," I said, unlatching myself. "Whatever is best for my girl."

"And you can use this for added comfort next time," she says, handing me a gauze bandeau. "Just wrap this around your chest and cut a slit out for each breast. It will hold the suction cups in place so you can pump hands-free."

"It's so pretty," I remark, realizing I just exchanged all my J. Crew bikinis for a burlap bandeau. I'm beginning to realize that fashion standards get swapped for pure functionality on this planet. As I reach to accept her bandeau offering, my elbow hits the bedside table, knocking over my pumping bounty.

"I'm so sorry!" I cry, as I watch all my liquid gold slowly soak into the pastel hospital sheets.

"There were a million different stem cells in that colostrum," she says. "You can't ever get that back." Her eyes glaze over again and cover with a yellowish hue. Her gaze penetrates mine, eyes-locked, as though she's trying to infect me with something.

And then, BOOM, it hits. Like a religious experience gone wrong, I'm shrouded in a finely woven baby blanket of MOM GUILT. In an instant, I watch all my child's college dreams fly out the window. No longer will she be smart, healthy, or a proper plastic-recycling citizen. I've decapitated all her stem cells.

"That will teach you, won't it?" she whispers as she leaves the room, assuredly teleporting back to the Mothership.

Long gone is the warm afterglow of birth. I'm frozen in an out-of-body experience. My daughter will now fail life, never learn to read, likely take up pole dancing or arson, all because of this moment. I dumped all her stem cells.

I turn to my husband for comfort and he shrugs, unsure what to say. Maybe the nurse is right? Maybe I've wrecked it! I close my eyes and hold my child, wondering what all just happened. I click my heels together three times. I want to go home. There's no place like home. There's no place like . . .

◆◆◆◆◆

MOTHERHOOD: DAY ONE: THREE HOURS LATER

"Why are you pumping?" a voice says from behind the hospital room curtain.

"Who's there?" I mutter. I can't handle further abductions. All I want to do is rest, but every few minutes, a new face appears with more devices and paperwork. First, it's the nurse to test baby's hearing. Then it's the baby name guy who works for the county; we don't have a name yet, meaning he will return in a few hours. Another nurse follows to check my vitals. A third nurse arrives to help me hobble to the bathroom. And all of them smile, beam at the baby, and advise me to "rest."

Why, I'd love to get some rest, dear hospital staff, but you interrupt me every time I close my eyes. Never wake a sleeping mama, isn't that rule numero uno?

This time it's our pediatrician. "Sorry to be so abrupt," she says, "but why are you pumping already?"

"I need my milk to come in. That's what the lactation nurse told me."

"Your milk will come in on its own."

"Even if I spilled my colostrum?" I ask.

"Your body will make it again. Do you want to pump?"

"Not really."

"Then you should stop."

"But isn't it good for the baby?"

"Your body knows what to do. You don't need to milk yourself. Let the baby do that."

And so begins the never-ending battle of contradictory mothering advice. Guilty if you pump. Guilty if you don't. Either way, guilty as a mother clam.

◆◆◆◆◆

SEPTEMBER 28: HOME FROM HOSPITAL

She's here! Meet Isa . . . 7 pounds, 6 ounces of bliss.

She's amazing! I'm so happy for you. And now our girls are officially three weeks apart! How was the birth?

I'll call you later to fill you in on all the details.

How are YOU?

I'm chaffed like a sandpapered leaf.

Which pads are you using?

The foot-long ones that attach to those see-through panties. The hospital collection.

Oh yes, I love that fall line.

Large enough to have a party in. Although there is no party happening over here. Ever. Again.

Oh, you just wait. Wait, where are you?

We just got home from the hospital. I can't believe they let us drive her home. They didn't even check our driving records. It took us half an hour to get up the courage to leave the parking lot and get on the highway.

It's crazy they trust us with these little lives.

It's pretty wild.

Did the hospital send you home with a bunch of goodies?

No, but I stole a bunch of those mesh panties from our ward.

You wouldn't be the first.

Oh, Ali Wong taught me how . . . Wait, baby girl's crying. Talk later. Love you.

So happy for you! Call me anytime. I'm definitely an expert now that I'm three weeks in. #Not #I'mSo'90sHip #ThatMakesMeNearly40

♦♦♦♦♦

SEPTEMBER 30

That's it. I'm quitting the sisterhood of women.

What's wrong?

I thought birth was supposed to be the hard part. Birth was easy compared to this. I can't even walk to the bathroom without a cane. Why did no one warn me about this?

It's awful. It's the cruelest thing women do to each other, talking about the birth as though that's the finish line. Labor starts when you get home!

I literally can't dismount my bed without help. My stomach muscles have officially turned in their pink slip. Once I even get to the ground, I can't walk right. I'm a hobbler!

You mean, a rodeo star?

My legs don't close anymore; I'm permanently stuck at ten centimeters. Plus, these darn maxi-pads are so wide, I swear they're causing me to dilate again.

I'm so sorry.

By the time I make it to the bathroom, then it's a different nightmare. There's a reason I dropped out of pre-med; I can't look at my own bodily fluids, and now there are open wounds to compete with.

And there's more to come.

Tell me EVERYTHING.

I tried to warn you with the perineum cream suggestion, but I didn't want to scare you out of birth. I needed a friend in the trenches with me.

I'm in the trench. When can we un-trench?

Never.

Yeah, there's no return button, is there?

It's the strangest feeling.

So, how are you holding up?

Well, I wasn't expecting this much love.

Me neither. It's crazy. I'm obsessed with her.

Me too. And then there's my nipples, which are SO sore. She vacuums them into chalk tubes.

Oh, I'm buying stock in lanolin cream.

You should. But the love is HUGE.

And it's not metaphorical. My chest is literally expanding with love, like the Grinch film. I woke up with two rock hard boulders hanging off my body.

Yes, apparently we now show our love with milk production. You have to massage the hard parts, or the milk gets blocked inside.

What if the whole thing is the hard part?

Then massage the whole thing. My boobs are a few weeks ahead of yours. They aren't hard anymore; now they just leak everywhere. I feel like a high-end drip irrigation system.

Wait, the milk doesn't just come out of the nipple?

No, there are like fifty different spouts.

The things they don't teach you in health class.

Or birth class.

Right? Even that placenta. Everyone was like, "Oh, once you push the baby out, the placenta will be easy."

Lies from hell. That was like adding a surprise 5k to a marathon.

You didn't encapsulate your placenta, did you?

No, I have to draw the line somewhere. I have friends that blendered theirs though.

Yeah, I can only be so organic when it comes to placentas.

We will heal up in a few days too. Unless that's another lie.

It can't be. We will feel healthy, and they are healthy, and then we'll have all the time in the world to focus on our new princesses.

So grateful they are healthy.

And then we have months off of work to do long walks and visit art museums . . .

And all the things that normal life doesn't afford.

Maternity leave. I bet it's almost like a sabbatical.

◆◆◆◆◆

Nearly all postpartum care products were designed by men, because they are neither comfortable nor cute.

Take, for example, those hospital-grade mesh panties I've been sporting for a week. Now there's a real winner. Sure, the giant gauze sling works, preventing my organs from falling out of the freshly paved ravine between my legs. But mesh? Women want to feel like fertility goddesses, not war heroes. I want silk and champagne, not bandages wrapped around my woo.

Then there's the hospital conditioner—another epic man fail. At some point after birth, you want to shower. Sure, it's a long waddle to that tub, but once there, it's like you've arrived at Mecca. God envelopes you through the full spiritual refreshment of the showerhead. But hospital conditioner obliterates that little slice of heaven; in fact, it's downright evil. I spent my first shower as a mother fighting tangles rather than refreshing my soul. Seriously, paraben-free Paul Mitchell conditioner needs to be on your packing list. You can thank me later. Oh, and enjoy every warm drop; it's the last solitary shower you'll get for a year.

After the shower, it's time for male-designed product numero three: the foot-long maxi pad. If a foot-long epidural wasn't enough, there are foot-long pads for your foot-long panties. The top of the pad starts at your belly button and the back wraps around to your shoulder blade. Be sure to stick the adhesive on correctly because, if you have not properly "installed" it and you wiggle, the adhesive sticks to all the wrong things. And it's just wrong. Bad, wrong story.

No woman would design these products, but women are not off scot-free either, as no woman actually warned me what I REALLY needed on my baby registry. I spent all my time fantasizing over wooden Montessori toys and organic muslin cloths, when I really should have registered for the following:

1. *A hot in-home masseuse. My body aches all over from the Dean-Kar-nazes-marathon of birth I just ran, and yours will too. Every muscle you never knew you had will ache, and there's no spa in sight. Register for a masseuse, the hotter the better. Better yet, send your partner to massage therapy school as soon as the pee stick gives you the plus sign. It's the least they can do while you bravely ensure the family lineage is carried on.*

2. *A hotter in-home chef. We are creeping into the fantasy realm here, but a girl can dream. Have them cook you lots of eggs because they give you choline and Omega-3s, which boost your mood from maniac to maniac-light. Better yet, send your husband to culinary school and remind him how hot he is every time he scrambles eggs. Then remind him that's the only egg of yours he can EVER get near again, and he needs to find a new purpose for his special purpose.*

3. *Your mother. Register for her. This is who you will actually import when the hot masseuse and chef don't show. She will help you with everything, and you will spend your early days in Momlandia wondering why you ever gave her any speck of grief.*

4. *A neck pillow, that u-shaped kind you buy at the airport. Bring this to the hospital as you will need it for the car ride home, but not for your neck. Prop it under you with the opening to the back. Post-baby car bumps don't mix with woo stitches, and the neck pillow has that perfect matching center hole. Pretend you are going on an exotic safari as you grab your neck pillow and fly.*

5. *Hemorrhoid cream. When you have a baby, God buys you a donut but not the kind you want. It's a cruel joke of nature that no one admits, but this cream will prevent unnecessary 911 calls each time your digestion cycle completes. Get the kind with the applicator end and turn on Deep-ak Chopra meditations while you use it. It's strangely transcendental.*

6. *Laxatives. Yup—stock up on Metamucil. The baby is the last thing you will ever want to push out for a while. Keep it uber relaxed and chill, girls. Sexy is as sexy does.*

7. *A squirt bottle. Post-baby, you won't be able to wipe for weeks. There's no way to make this part sexy, honey, but think of it as your own portable bidet.*

8. *A pocket purse fan. I bought the cat version with kitten ears just to keep things fun. Turn the handheld fan to the highest setting and wave it*

*around to dry yourself down there. Don't get the moving blades too close
to anything that matters.*

9. *Organic tush cream. For you. The baby won't need theirs for weeks. You
   will need yours pronto.*

10. *Organic diapers. For you. The baby's diapers will be tiny, and you will be
    gifted plenty. Your diapers will be large enough to house a small country,
    and no one will ever buy them for you.*

11. *Champagne. Wine. More champagne and wine. Deep breaths, Ladies.*

♦♦♦♦♦

OCTOBER 3

*Okay, I need to speed-dial this healing down there. The diapers have
gotta go.*

I've got the woo part down to a three-step process.

I like systems.

I'll send you a diagram if you want. For the top, use that perineum
balm. For the middle part, witch hazel pads.

Witch hazel? I haven't heard that word since teenage breakouts.

Witch hazel those babies. For the back part, Preparation H with aloe.

This is ridiculous.

And sit on a pillow at ALL times. Have you tried sitz baths yet?

Aren't those for the elderly?

Well, anyone over thirty-five is technically a geriatric mother.

A high-risk geriatric mother.

Watch out. This is about to get risqué.

♦♦♦♦♦

*In case you've never shopped for a sitz bath, they are not in the baby aisle
of CVS. They are in the nursing home aisle, along with most other products
you will need postpartum. You see, having a baby not only gives you a farm of
crow's feet you didn't sign up for, but it also switches the aisle where you shop.*

Lingerie . . . out.

Adult Depends . . . SO IN.

*While motherhood kindly pushes you to the denture section, mother-
hood also bans you from anti-aging products. Retinol? Those chemicals hurt*

the baby. Eye creams? Maybe next year. So, at the pinnacle of your tiredness and in the era where you most rapidly age, all the beauty products that revive you are off limits.

What's in your cart now? A sitz bath with a bonus bidet squirter for those special angles.

Drawing a sitz bath is a delicate art. You fill the mini-tub with warm water, add the organic herb blend you ordered from Etsy, and then gently place the tub into the toilet's seat. The first time I tried, I didn't draw enough water for my bath, so sitting did nothing. It felt more like squatting in an open-air garden. So, then I added more water—too much water, ultimately—and liquid spilled all over the floor.

It's a tender balance, aging is.

When you fill the bath right, it's the closest thing to a retreat you'll get in the first weeks postpartum. I put on Spa Pandora, lit a candle, dimmed the lights, and settled into my tub-on-a-toilet throne. For a real zen experience, add lavender salts to the tub. The lavender lets you sort-of forget that you are salting an open wound. Inhale lavender, exhale healing, and prepare for total relaxation.

Until your baby starts crying. You see, babies have a built-in sitz bath detector. Every time you sit on that mini-tub, your baby will cry from the next room, which means your boobs will start their irrigation cycle. Which means your darling husband will magically appear with babe in arms, asking, "Don't you want to feed the baby?"

At this point, you have two options. Nurse the child on the toilet (never fun) or grab your stolen hospital panties, drip dry (since your pocket fan is not within grasp), and then go nurse your darling.

Since when did motherhood become so graphic? I feel like an NC-17 film that babies should not watch. This healing part, frankly, should be banned. When I get to heaven, I'm asking God why humans can't just lay eggs. We can sit on them, keep them warm, and then when our chicklings peck their way out, we would have the energy to hold them. I mean, birds really have this parenting thing down; I've never seen them sporting sitz baths. Humans, take note!

◆◆◆◆◆

OCTOBER 6

My feet are on fire. It feels like someone is stabbing needles in them. *What? What do feet have to do with postpartum?*

Apparently, I can thank all the hormonal changes since birth, as my doctor says it's normal.

Motherhood = pain = normal?

Deceptively so. I'm now wearing orthotics and Asics.

Sexy.

So, I'm now alternating foot baths and icing, and going to the podiatrist and PT twice a week to recover.

Does it help?

It barely touches the pain.

I'm still confused. How in the world does motherhood affect our feet?

It affects everything. Hot flashes are fun too.

Oh, I had those a couple of nights ago. Night sweats.

Changed the meaning of the word "sweatpants" for me.

Is this ALL from the hormone changes?

Yes, it's how our bodies evolve into caring beings. We can care for whole villages if we wanted.

My boobs prove it. I got out of the shower the other day and BOOM! Projectile milk all over the tile walls.

See, we are goddesses of milk.

Virile feminine wonderlands. Shoot, I just sneezed. What the HECK?

Need a change of clothes? Mothers can't sneeze, laugh, or wait in long lines for the bathroom anymore. File those all in "former life" categories.

If men gave birth, they would give themselves medals for this.

Medals of Honor.

Meanwhile, we birth and raise civil humans without a glance!

Preach.

My award can be paid out in flowers. Massages. House cleaners. And thin mints.

Amen.

I'm calling the Norwegian Nobel Prize Committee and asking that every mother be awarded the highest honors.

Oh, don't worry. The state pays maternity leave at fifty-five percent for twelve weeks, which is enough to buy nappies and Motrin.

Now, that's noble if I ever heard it.

◆◆◆◆◆

OCTOBER 7

So, I bought Isa all gender-neutral baby clothes as I can't stand pink or purple.

Neither can I.

We now have a closet full of beige and grey clothes. There's only one problem. My child is a spring palette. She's one giant ball of rosy cheeks.

Get used to it. They will defy all of our wishes throughout their whole lives.

I thought I was being woke, but grey washes her out. I have to embrace it. Pink is her color.

Speaking of embracing, have you tried the Haakaa? It's some kind of natural milk catcher. You cup it on one boob while you nurse the baby on the other. My super hippy pediatrician told me about it.

What does it do?

It catches the extra milk from your boob not in use.

So, you hold the baby with one arm and the funnel with the other?

Exactly. Football hold each one.

And which hand holds the water bottle? I'm guzzling gallons these days. It's insatiable. I've never been so thirsty in my life.

And the thirst keeps growing.

I'm considering wearing my extreme sports Camelback around the house.

Do it. Motherhood is the most extreme sport I've ever played.

I just ordered a bunch of sports bras off of Target too. See, we are SPORTY.

Look how athletic we are! What other adventure gear do we need?

I need a Sherpa to carry all my piles of laundry from the floor to the washing machine.

Ooh, maybe he can even set the cycles too.

And switch the laundry to the dryer.

And fold.

Stop! This fantasy is too much.

Remember when romance looked like long walks on the beach?

And now it looks like the laundromat.

A laundromat full of PINK clothes. Sigh.

♦♦♦♦♦

OCTOBER 8

So, my county has a program where you get a free visit from a lactation consultant.

Free? That's amazing. I had three different ones at the hospital. I owe them my life.

My lactation consultant at the hospital mom-shamed me.

As though motherhood wasn't hard enough without our own kin turning on us. What did she say?

I pumped and spilled the milk. She told me that would teach me.

She sounds like someone who lives under a rock.

Yes, a giant breast-shaped boulder.

This one will be different. Can she come to your house?

Yes, and as soon as we meet, I'll take off my shirt. I'll give consent, and then she will touch my breasts.

Everything about motherhood defies everything we've ever been taught about modesty and all constructs of privacy. My body is no longer my own.

Then whose is it?

Good question.

◆◆◆◆◆

OCTOBER 9: LACTATION CONSULTANT VISITATION

Hi Margaret! Welcome to my home.

Hi Jennifer! Thank you for having me. I know it can be a little awkward having strangers in your home just a few days after birth, but whatever I can do to make you more comfortable, just let me know.

It's all going really well. No complaints here.

That's amazing. No pain?

Well, maybe a little, but I foam rolled it out last night.

Have you tried turmeric? That can help with postpartum inflammation. Take a teaspoon of powdered turmeric with a couple of ounces of orange juice every three hours.

I actually have turmeric, but the bottle said, "Check with your doctor if pregnant or breastfeeding."

It's very common to see that phrase on relatively safe medicines. The infant risk center categorizes turmeric as an L3 risk, which means there's limited research on it. But honestly, it's consumed all over the world as a spice and generally recognized as safe.

Anything without a warning label at all?

Yes. You can also put cold cabbage leaves on any nursing pain or swelling. Speaking of, how is breastfeeding going?

She's latching pretty well.

Good. Keep making the sandwich with your hand to help her latch.

What sandwich? I haven't had a sandwich in weeks!

You want to make a sandwich of your breast. Just grab your breast in between your thumb and pointer finger and squeeze around your nipple. Do you want me to show you?

Oh, and there you are! How long do we sandwich?

Keep sandwiching as long as nursing still doesn't feel great. Anything else I can help you with while I'm here?

I'm sooo good. Truly, spectacularly good.

Do you want me to watch you nurse?

Sure, we can do that if we need to.

Great, why don't you get the baby unswaddled and ready. In the meantime, I want to remind you of the Mother's Circle every Wednesday at the hospital. You may find it helpful to breastfeed in the group with other moms. It can be freeing to see how everyone does it.

◆◆◆◆◆

OCTOBER 9: LATER ON

I just sent a picture of my nipple to my lactation consultant.

OMG.

Isn't this sexting or something?

Did you feel sexy as you sent it?

Um, the exact opposite. There's nothing sensual left to my body.

Not sexting.

She promised to delete it. Still bizarre. I felt so awkward nursing with her. It's my first female grope.

That's her job to help you nurse.

I know. It still feels weird to have strangers squish your nipples.

True, and sending breast pics is weird, even for medical reasons. But mostly because it's new. I guess this is mothering in 2019.

I need other pictures to clear my mind. Send me one! I want to see your little one.

(Picture sent)

She's so adorable, Sam. You made a gem. Here's mine.

(Picture sent)

Love her. Squish her cheeks!

Yours too. I hope mine keeps her pout lips. I think it's her best quality, along with her turquoise eyes. We aren't too sure about her baldness, but it's a work in progress.

She can borrow Enora's hair. She came out like Elvis. We are hoping some of her extra fur goes away.

Here's one more pic.

I think that's the boob pic you sent the lactation consultant.

Oh my goodness, I'm sorry!

Looks like a good one to me! Nothing to be ashamed of there.

◆◆◆◆◆

Before children, manicures were a highlight of relaxation. A special treat. A Saturday morning indulgence.

Post-children, manicures are solely reserved for your infant. You don't have time for one, but your darling baby will need one every few days. Their angel-brushed nails are daggers, and they take every opportunity to claw at their angel-kissed cheeks, sometimes so deeply you speed dial the plastic surgeon.

"Put socks on her hands!" a friend told me, which worked for a few days. Then another mom saw the socks and told me I was cruel. "Babies love exploring the world with their fingers; don't inhibit their joys!" And so, I'm back to the manicures.

Manicures are only possible while the baby girl is sleeping. You hover over her bassinet, lift her microscopic palm, and hope for the best—the procedure a delicate balance between trimming princess' nails and avoiding digit amputation.

To perform the circus-act of close manicures, regular clippers won't do. You need tiny fairy scissors that wrap around your pinky. Then, you take baby on a drive until she passes out cold. Pull over, creak open the backseat car door, and lift each of her fingers one by one for the glamour clips. On-the-road manis are the only true option. Or socks . . . those cruel, cruel socks which sound enormously easy to me right now.

Because easy is just too, well, easy for the new mom.

◆◆◆◆◆

OCTOBER 10

Okay, back to breastfeeding. Do you use an app to track your feeds?

Yes, I log everything. Don't ask what I'll do with all that info, but it feels so good to log.

I was looking at a few feeding apps today. The one I downloaded has a strange logo; it's an upside-down C. I can't tell if it's a deflated breast or a condom.

Definitely the former.

After feeding Isa all night long, I say condom. I think the app is sending subliminal messages to wear protection.

You aren't doing that yet, are you?

Oh God, no!

Wait, you aren't wearing protection?

No, we aren't doing it yet.

Thank God. I told my husband my doctor hasn't cleared me.

I'll tell my doctor to never clear me at this rate.

I hear the sex drive comes back eventually. Babies get siblings somehow, right?

Yes, I hear wine makes lots of babies.

♦♦♦♦♦

OCTOBER 11

Have you heard of nipple confusion?

Oh yes, it's totally real. If you give babies too many nipples, they get confused and quit life.

And nobody likes a baby who quits life.

Nobody! That's why we haven't tried a bottle yet with Enora. We don't want to confuse her.

So, my doctor says nipple confusion is a sham. She says babies are smart enough to know what's a breast and what's not, and they won't quit breastfeeding if you give them a bottle. Babies can do both.

So, nipple confusion isn't real?

According to her. My mom is laughing at me as I type this.

My mom also. I swear she thinks I'm nuts, but I'm so grateful she's here. She is going to live with us for the next two months.

My mom is here with us too right now. I honestly couldn't do it without her, even though she rolls her eyes at all my Googling.

All the parenting advice keeps changing! When my mom had her babies, all the hospitals said babies sleep on their tummies. Now it's the "back to sleep" movement because of SIDS.

Right? And then there's the whole breastfeeding saga. My mom formula-fed me, as that was all the rage then. Now, the hospital scared me away from using bottles at all. They sold us on this tiny syringe contraption. I pump and then use the syringe to scoop up a few drops of milk to place on Isa's tongue.

You syringe feed her? Isn't that for baby rescue animals?

And organic babies, obviously. But yes, we syringe feed her for the 1 a.m. night feed. That's Jeff's bonding time.

That's the time I'm elbowing Mateo over here too.

But my doctor laughed at us today and said to just give her a bottle.

Did you?

I did. It was terrifying as she's been latching so well, I was petrified to disturb the peace.

And . . . ?

NO NIPPLE CONFUSION!

Ah, the agony.

You have no idea. I recommend it.

I'm not sure if we can make the leap.

Oh, I'm also in love with my new lactation consultant. We've been texting daily. She has lots of good pics in her pocket by now.

I want to invite mine over for Christmas. By then, I might be wearing shirts again.

What's a shirt? I've abandoned them.

Thrown them out the window.

Topless mothers for the win. You know what's just dumb? Putting on a shirt! I have to take it off every hour to feed anyway, and when I do wear one, she spits up on it.

Maybe we should just cut two holes in a t-shirt. That way we won't be naked, but our littles can have instant access.

Glamorous. Back to nipple confusion.

Okay, I will trust you. Bottles here we come.

Your child is the offspring of two Ivy leaguers. I think she'll master this SAT question.

Which nipple is not real? Circle all that apply.

You've got this!

♦♦♦♦♦

OCTOBER 12

The bottle worked! She gobbled that pumped milk right up. This is a whole new world! My husband can now take the midnight shift. That's a full 10 p.m.-2 a.m. sleep for me.

Hallelujah, Jesus is risen.

You know you are sleep deprived when a four-hour stretch sounds like a five-star hotel.

I'd settle for any hours. I can't fall asleep at all.

No!

I've been putting off saying it out loud, but I can't sleep a wink. It started a few weeks before birth, but I thought I was just excited about the baby. Well, the baby is definitely here now, and I'm still not sleeping.

Have you talked to the doctor?

I go back in a few weeks. I don't feel depressed though.

I'm depressed that you aren't sleeping. Try acupuncture. Those little needles do wonders.

◆◆◆◆◆

OCTOBER 13

The acupuncturist cured me!

Eureka! You found a solution.

Yes, although the effects are wearing off. But boy, those were a good few sleeps.

How's Isa's sleep?

Oh, she's still up every three hours.

Can you go back to the acupuncturist?

I can try. I may need to learn how to prick myself.

I have my first acupuncture appointment tomorrow too. I still feel like I'm walking on pins and needles all the time.

Ouch. I can't even . . .

So, ironically, I'm going to try sticking ACTUAL needles in my feet to cure the pain.

This is warfare.

Gettysburg right on our bodies.

Do you think this is just a later mom thing? Surely the twenty-year-olds don't go through this body combat.

I'm sure they bounce back like Ping Pongs. That's why moms under forty birth siblings for their kids.

◆◆◆◆◆

Dear Friends,

Stop buying me baby tchotchkes.

Seriously. The absolute ugliest thing you can do for a mom is buy her baby gadgets. Life is hard enough.

I know you mean well, but cut it out.

You won't know this until you are a mom. But the worst thing you can do is send a mother lots of packages in that beautiful window of the first month of her baby's life—that gorgeous span of time when her butt is puffing, her boobs are leaking, her partner has gone back to work, and she is home alone with a baby that poops three thousand times a day.

That is the time to pause. Refrain from your own shopping urges. I know it's not as cute as a onesie, but please drop off a warm meal or fold some laundry or come hold the baby for an hour. Or even twenty minutes.

But please, refrain from presents.

Whatever you do, do NOT send the baby a gift.

As I write this, I feel guilty, knowing that many of my beautiful friends sent me beautiful gifts. I do not overtly hate you. I'm most appreciative. But STOP already.

I repeat, a new mom does not have time to unpack more gifts, return duplicates to UPS, put away mountains of toys, and crush Amazon boxes for recycling. She only has time to exist. And when there's a gift, there's a thank-you card to send, and that just mounts too much pressure, particularly since all the other moms have thank-you cards in the mail faster than Amazon Prime. So that makes me feel even worse. I am now behind on thanking you for the gift I don't have time to open. If there is a baby two, please send all presents during pregnancy when the illusion of time still exists.

And Grandmas, WE LOVE YOU and your helpful gifts, but every time you get the online Target urge, how about dropping the twenty in a college fund instead? My child does not need any more hot pink Hot Wheels. She needs an education. In fact, maybe Target will partner with me—you select a gift from their website, they take a cut, you get a picture receipt of the shiny toy you want to overrun my house with, and the rest gets funneled into a 529 plan. Every penny helps.

In gratitude,

Jennifer

♦♦♦♦♦

OCTOBER 14

Ever feel like you can no longer make eye contact with the neighbors?
Oh, I stopped looking at them a long time ago. They've witnessed too many atrocities.
I wonder how many times they've seen me in my disposable hospital underwear?
Or seen me nursing while scarfing down flax muffins.
Well, you are making nutrients for two.
Yes, we are raising strong societies on our milk.
I'm still never looking at the neighbors again.

♦♦♦♦♦

OCTOBER 15

I got your birth announcement. She is absolutely stunning.
Isn't she cute?
Here's what I really want to know, though. How in the world did you have time to make, mail, and post actual cards? I'm still mastering the illustrious skill called "brushing my hair."
I did the cards while my Mom was still here.
You are so on-point.
Sweetheart, of course I am. I'm half-Korean. That's why you need ethnic friends.
To remind me how lazy my white tush is? Probably.
Just skip the birth announcements. You put it on Facebook, didn't you?
That doesn't count. What if I just send Instagram birth announcements. Is that a thing?
You could start a trend.

♦♦♦♦♦

OCTOBER 16

How is it without your mom?

SO MUCH HARDER. She's only gone for the week, but I'm trying to convince her to move in full-time. I can't believe I'm saying that.

Oh, my mother and I turned a whole new leap once my baby was born. We get along WAY better now. She focuses on the baby, and it magically makes all my flaws disappear in her eyes. I have given her a grandchild! Plus, having her here is the only way I can get anything done, and by getting anything done, I mostly mean showering.

Does the husband like living with the MIL?

They like each other more than they like me. Didn't I tell you what her dinner commentary was the other night? I was a mess, covered in cooking spices, laying dinner on the table for my sweet family, and in enters my showered mother and well-kept husband. And he offers to change the baby's diaper and my mother looks at me and beams, "He's the whole package."

Did you tell her how many diapers you'd already changed that day?

Oh, this hasn't just happened once. It's become her nightly mantra. "Jen, he's the WHOLE package." I told her, "Mom, please stop talking about my husband's package."

Maybe the awe is generational. I bet many women in her era rarely saw a baby hold a baby.

You mean, rarely saw a man hold a baby?

Freudian slip.

♦♦♦♦♦

OCTOBER 17

So just after I sent out my birth announcement, I came across this 2017 *New Yorker* article on realistic baby announcements by Riane Konc. Here are a few of my favorites:

"Welcome to the world, little one! Mom and baby just survived the most traumatic event of their lives thus far, so for some reason, Dad is recovering.

"World, meet Eveline! Mommy was such a champ and is, unbeknownst to Daddy, newly celibate.

"Jordan and I are so happy to share the birth of our girls. They are healthy and happy, and we have never been more in love, if love is what you call it when you realize that all the ants you've ever stomped on also had mothers and then you just sob and sob."

These are brilliant. I'm inspired to make mine now. "Welcome to the world, Isa! It only took two laborious days to meet you, but everyone tells me I will forget those feelings . . . I haven't, I adore you, find me on the sitz bath."

Awesome. Should I resend mine saying, "Enora, you are worth every penny. And now I have no pennies, since I plan to send you to college in 2035."

At least it's honest.

◆◆◆◆◆

So, it's not as though our current generation was the first to ever go organic or have natural childbirths or champion breastfeeding. The '70s hit well before us, and long before that, women all over the globe have roamed topless through their villages, feeding babies with their golden breastmilk. Nothing they did was touted as "natural." They ate their crops because the tomatoes sprouted in their yards. They squatted on birthing rocks in the middle of streams while their tribes sang victory songs around them.

It was as intuitive as it gets.

But it takes us Westerners a little longer to pick up on things, remarket them, and elevate them to hipster status. Take yoga, for example. Twenty years ago, we imported stretches from India while inviting the TRULY spiritual to don Lululemon pants . . . because spandex definitely connects you to the divine. Now many of us who rode the yoga wave in our twenties are having kids in our thirties.

And there's a lot of pressure to do it right.

Now, you must have the right raw amber teething necklace and eco-friendly non-plastic toys and Montessori wooden everything. And you must post pictures of your baby in their organic cotton outfit on Instagram just to show how easy it all looks. And baby slings! You need the right new-fangled circle cloth to match your child's bamboo outfit.

Newsflash: None of this is new! Montessori wooden toys are just age-old forest sticks. Millennial moms did not invent the Ergo; baby wraps have been around for centuries. Breastfeeding benefits are not new science, despite how often the WHO updates its guidelines. Women have been churning out babies since the beginning of time, and we are simply repurposing our ancestors' wisdom.

But now, there's not-so-subtle pressure to be a card-carrying member of this ancient mothering tribe. Now, you not only have to be a woke mom, you also have to be up on all the latest trends while reaching into the indigenous past. Moms must now be farmers, chefs, and knitters. Moms should grow the baby, grow baby's food, and feed baby the freshest milk supply in the land. And then, once again, she must put it all on social media, next to the homemade baby organic puree she made her from chia seed scratch.

One by one, other moms will comment on her feed, reminding her how amazing she is. And what remains silent is the thousands of other moments that aren't picture-worthy. Those hours filled with spit-ups and baby cries and mom tears. But no one wants to broadcast that or admit that online. And so, we pull ourselves up by our bootstraps and knead our sourdough bread, one flax-seed muffin at a time.

And sometimes, I eat the whole batch.

♦♦♦♦♦

OCTOBER 18:

Have you started tummy time?

Starting now. I just discovered that Enora LOVES sleeping on her tummy, which I know is a no-no. But if I supervise her, I think it's okay.

Jeff wombs her sometimes. I think that counts as tummy time, right?

What's wombing?

He puts her in that bandeau the hospital gave us and wears her on his chest. But she's on her tummy while on his chest.

Yes, that counts because she's working her neck and back muscles. Wearing her in the Ergo also counts.

Maybe I need some tummy time.

What's a tummy?

Exactly. I can't find mine. I still look six months pregnant. It's like my liver had a baby.

It will shrink. #thoughtsandprayers

Sure it will.

#prayersandwine

♦♦♦♦♦

OCTOBER 19

Does Enora grunt?

Like a piglet.

Mine too. Is that normal?

I'm not sure. It may be reflux.

Will she grow out of it?

No, I think she will sound like a pig her whole life.

Perfect. Glad I was in FFA as a kid.

I'll buy you a blue ribbon. Best grunter.

Can I get a bumper sticker for that? Proud parent of a precious piglet.

Yes, but only if you put it right next to lots of Ivy league bumper stickers.

Oh, I already plan to decorate my car with obnoxious signs from Princeton, Yale, and Stanford, but secretly, I hope she cashes in on our community college. It's free and the top in the nation.

I'll get you a bumper sticker for that too. Community college, Harvard-grad, Grunter.

#MomDreams

◆◆◆◆◆

OCTOBER 20

First projectile poop. All over the white bed frame.

Awesome. Whose idea was the white bed frame?

But it looked so pretty, Sam.

With poo on it?

I'm still in denial that children are messy. Can't I train her to be clean?

Enora projectile vomited twice last night. Scared the shat out of us. It went all over the house.

Time to cover the whole farm with wee-wee pads. Did I tell you I also got white couches? It made so much sense while pregnant.

Most things do. Supposedly, the spit-up is normal at this age, but it's only happened for us when she's eaten too much. She's also burping a lot these days; way more than a few weeks ago. She's like an old woman.

How old is she now?

You would think she's ninety, but she's only six weeks.

Mine's almost four. Still crying a bunch.

We definitely hit a fussy stage. The doctor said these next few weeks can be super challenging as their digestive system develops—as though the other weeks aren't?

◆◆◆◆◆

OCTOBER 21

What carrier are you wearing in your Instagram story?

The way-too-large Baby K'Tan. I must have bought the wrong size as it sags down to my belt. I also have the Moby wrap. Have you tried that? It seems a bit complicated.

There's no way I'll tie that right. I failed origami in high school. #babygirldropsonfloor

Seriously, it's longer than my car, and you just keep wrapping it around yourself until it secures the baby.

Yeah, I don't trust myself with that apparatus.

I think I spent over forty hours researching baby carriers. That's a full week of work on this project, and now I'm more confused than ever. The most expensive ones just seem like a large piece of cloth.

They are. We went into the wrong industry.

Apparently so. Ninety dollars for a cotton square that I have to tie to myself.

So really, it's just a pricey scarf.

That every mom buys.

Speaking of carriers, I'm holding her right now and it's working!

What's working?

My arms are! I'm attempting my first mom outing to the salon. I'm liter-ally getting a cheap pedicure right now while she sleeps on my chest. My mom came with too. It's a full girl party.

See, that's way easier than a carrier. Plus, your arms are attached so she can't fall out.

Most days.

◆◆◆◆◆

OCTOBER 22

I've entered the land of plugged ducts.

Oh no! That sounds like a bad plumbing problem.

Correct. Please send Drano. I'm literally sitting on the couch with an open diaper on each boob.

And that . . . ?

Steams out the plugged pores. I soaked the diapers in hot water first and the steam dislodges the plugs.

Sexy as heaven.

We are sporting so many hot looks these days.

I have back fat all of a sudden, right behind my shoulder blades. It's full-on handlebars. Grabbable.

Fancy.

I also just bought a scale.

Why in the land of Moses would you do that?

Because I dropped twenty pounds the first week, I was so excited. Then I gained weight, and I was not so excited.

Well, I can squeeze back in my jeans if I use rubber bands around the waist button. That counts, right? But I've also grown these saggy new pouches under my arms. Apparently, they are a very strange part of the upper mammary glands.

Welcome to mammalhood! I actually just read that women's boobs don't fully develop until you have kids.

Is that what this is? I'm developing?

It's puberty part deux. With all those fun middle school hormone feelings.

Will you sign my yearbook?

Dear Sam, you are a rad mom. Stay cool. Never change. Except maybe those saggy arm pouches.

♦♦♦♦♦

OCTOBER 23

Husband is already talking baby two. I told him the factory is closed.

I scoffed when our pediatrician asked about baby two. Practically almost slapped her.

Is sex happening?

You're joking, right? The IUD is scheduled for two weeks . . . Did I tell you that Mateo got weirded out around six months into pregnancy? We paused intimacy. He thought things could hit the baby.

Ah, dear men have such big dreams. Our doctor prescribed us sex during the last month of pregnancy. We had to schedule it 4x a week.

Oh no. That's worse than no sex. Prescriptive sex.

Prescriptive pregnancy sex.

Not sexy.

Particularly when you weigh more than your husband who's already a foot taller than you.

♦♦♦♦♦

OCTOBER 24

Isa is one month old! I dressed her up in angel wings and took a cute photo next to a chalkboard.

As you should! We don't want to miss every month's birthday now, do we?

I know a mom that has her child's birthday outfits planned out already. For the entire year.

Her baby must be a total dud. Nobody has that kind of time.

True. Or she has a full-time nanny, photographer, and personal shopper.

Or that. I hate those moms. #jealous

◆◆◆◆◆

OCTOBER 25

Why do you live so far away?

I know. It would be like the good old college days when we got all dressed up and went out and danced. Only this time we would wear steamed diapers on our chests.

And Baby Bjorns as our dresses.

I'm thinking of going rogue. None of this glamour Patagonia mom stuff. I'm making over my Instagram to look momly. Let's put curlers in our hair . . .

Yes! And wear oversized sunglasses and slip-on jelly shoes and take up smoking.

And gorge on Dunkin' Donuts holes.

While binging on extra-sugared coffee in our Caddies. Now that's real motherhood.

Speaking of motherhood, did you join a mom group?

Should I?

I don't know. Isn't this enough?

Yes, but maybe it's some rite of passage that we are missing out on. You birth a baby, and you get a new tribe. That sounds cool, right?

Only if I get to drive the Caddy.

◆◆◆◆◆

As soon as you have a baby, you need to join a mom group, or at least, this was another piece of unsolicited advice from friends. Honestly, I never understood the hype. After all, I was thirty-nine years old. My high school girlfriends had high school children. My local girlfriends had toddlers. Sam and I texted all day. Surely, I was covered by both moms and groups.

But when you leave the hospital, you start getting pamphlets: PEP. Breastfeeding group. La Leche League. Mothers Who Sew All Their Clothes. Attachment Parenting Tribe. Postpartum Therapy Circle.

For the first few weeks, I said no. I didn't need a mom circle or yarn or therapy.

But then I suffered from my next inevitable case of mom guilt.

It started out more like FOMO. What was I missing here? Everyone else seemed to need this, so why was I exempt? And then it turned from FOMO to envy. Every other mom was leaving the house once a week for their mom group of choice. They were showering, putting shirts on, and entering the world with their babies.

How dare they do it without me!

And so, I grabbed the pamphlets and headed to my local PEP group. PEP stands for Postpartum Education Program. The brochure described it as an eight-week course to learn the art and science of mothering. It was held in an inviting church cafeteria and started just before lunch, which meant I could attempt being prompt.

This would be my first solo venture out with the baby, where I was solely responsible for her life. I would have to dress her, change her, strap her into the car seat, and drive us there. Who in the world gave me permission to do this? Sure, I'm an experienced educator, but that's different. Give me emotional teenagers any day. Babies are a whole other planet I've never bothered to visit. In fact, I never even viewed Planet Baby through a telescope. I skipped babysitting jobs in high school—way too vulnerable of a population. Humans that speak in full sentences? Now that's my jam. Cooing babies? Someone please translate. I'm definitely not that smart.

I entered the PEP room and was greeted by a circle of twenty-five moms and their littles. Most of the babies were roughly four months old, some in car seats on the floor, some in Ergos on their moms. The group leader started a discussion about returning to work after baby. I clearly was on the final presentation of the series, as I was the only one sporting a newborn.

After a few minutes, one baby started to cry. Then another. Then a third, until the room was in a dissonant symphony. It was unnerving, engulfing. I felt chills down my spine. And then I looked down and realized why I felt damp.

My shirt was completely drenched in two symmetric circles.

That was the moment I learned that my chest was now public property and responds to duty calls from all babies everywhere. Not only does my baby's cry make me flow, but any demanding baby will do. My unsuspecting body can churn gelato for any infant who asks.

The whole thing got overwhelming rather quickly. Between the unex-pected wet t-shirt contest and my own baby's hunger, I bolted for the door.

My first outing was a devious success.

♦♦♦♦♦

OCTOBER 26

I did my first stroller walk today to the post office to mail you my extra Moby wrap. I've learned how to tie it, and I think you can too. Anyway, en route, I discovered the real use for the bottom compartment of the stroller.

What's that?

It fits three wine bottles perfectly.

That's magical. Wine and post office? You are working it these days.

They were next to each other. It seemed like the perfect outing.

Oh, I'm a cheap date these days. Quarter glass, and I'm done.

Me too. Three bottles will last me until Christmas.

Just in time to make baby two.

Punch you.

♦♦♦♦♦

OCTOBER 27

Question: Does Enora cry all day?

What do you mean?

Your response says everything. I'm screwed.

I mean, she has a witching hour at dusk, but other than that, she's pretty chill.

Yeah, I've been blaming it on the witching hour, that witch is spreading into many hours.

Does anything help?

We take turns bouncing her when she gets out her broomstick.

How many hours are you in Oz?

Oh, six to eight hours each night.

That's a good thigh workout. Does she stop crying?

Not completely. I keep telling myself it's a fluke.

Have you tried baby massage yet?

Is that a thing?

I'll email you the video link. You basically write "I love you" on their tummies and it cures their gas problems.

I wish someone would write "I love you" on my stomach. Oh wait, I have no stomach.

Exactly. I've also tried laying Enora over my lap and lifting her bum in the air.

I don't wish someone would do that to me.

It helps the gas come out.

Which end?

The rear. And then I bicycle her legs when she's on her back.

This is a full workout.

Someone needs a workout!

God knows I'm not getting one right now.

◆◆◆◆◆

HOW TO ENSURE YOUR CRYING BABY STOPS CRYING

1. *Recruit Grandma, who does not believe sweet, innocent babies could possibly scream at all.*

2. *Leave the baby with Grandma for the morning while you resume some semblance of humanhood, like going grocery shopping and semi-brushing your hair.*

3. *Return home to a shiny happy baby who never made a peep, as crying babies emulate the Dali Lama when others are around, so others think you are the crazy one.*

4. *Listen as your mother tells you that you are overly paranoid, that your sweet-innocent-angel-baby did nothing but coo while you left, and you must be doing something wrong.*

5. *Thank Grandma for her sage advice and send her back to the grocery store. This not only reverses the experiment, but you also forgot the pacifier you went to the store for in the first place.*

6. *Watch your baby stare at you, give you the evil eye, flare her eyebrows, and start violently raging as soon as Grandma is out the door.*

7. *Eat an entire gallon of ice cream while bouncing your screaming baby. Be grateful you didn't forget the mint chip at the grocery store.*

8. *Smile when Grandma returns with a pacifier and watch your darling daughter stop screaming a good minute before Grandma crosses the doorway.*

9. *Watch Grandma cup your darling child in her arms, look at you, and say the dreaded words, "I told you so."*

♦♦♦♦♦

OCTOBER 28

My mom left back for Seattle today.

Solo mothering. That's awful . . . Well, we still have the husbands.

(Extended silence.)

How are you coping?

I make one tiny goal per day. Like washing my face. Or making dinner. Today's task: returning Amazon purchases.

I have a to-do list taped to my fridge. It's full of maternity leave goals, of which I've accomplished none.

Toss the list. It will only depress you.

But I need to remind myself I'm good at something besides laundry.

Oh, are you good at laundry?

No! I have no domestic qualities.

Do you like to cook?

Not really.

Do you like to clean?

Nope, but I hate dust, so I do it anyway. My full-time job right now is filled with things I'm not qualified for. The boss should fire me.

You are the boss.

Oh, right.

I'm learning motherhood is all about having lower expectations, a concept I suck at.

In the real world, if I checked off one item from my to-do list, I would feel wildly unproductive. Now here I am, holding my child, and she is my to-do list. But I can't check-her off because parenting will never be done.

It's a really hard balance. I mean, what do we do with the three decades before this? Do we pretend that didn't exist? Do we shelve those lives?

I haven't figured that out.

It's disturbing when I hear moms say they don't remember life before their baby.

Oh, the "I can't imagine life without her" speech.

Bite me. I fully remember my life. Those decades don't get erased!

I can DEFINITELY imagine my pre-baby life. With great fondness. I didn't have a child because life felt incomplete.

Does that make us bad moms?

Probably.

Yeah, I'm not raising my hand to admit that one.

When I hear those statements, I wonder if those women are telling the truth. And if they are, what's up that I DON'T feel that way?

Maybe we can be grateful our daughters are here AND grateful we lived before they came.

I sure hope so.

Or maybe life gets reprioritized and loving our little humans is our greatest accomplishment.

That sounds like a nice Hallmark card. I thought mothering later in life would answer some of those questions, but I feel like it complicates them.

It obscures our resumes, for sure.

Dream big, little daughters! Dream so big you can have a career and family, and maybe by then, society will have figured out how to let you have both!

Hey, you got a pedicure a few days ago! That's a big dream of mine right now.

True, although I had to excuse myself to the bathroom every ten minutes. I'm still not used to this new internal timer of mine.

Well, have you seen a diagram of how the baby rewired our bladders? This is why we run to the bathroom all the time. We don't have a choice. I'll send the image to you.

I actually saw that.

Facebook must be marketing the same sh*t to all new moms.

I'm sure of it. I used to get targeted ads for cute clothes. Now I'm marketed bladder diagrams.

From career clothes to bathroom charts.

Somehow our lives will all blend one day, right?

Time will tell.

◆◆◆◆◆

I am a bad mom for skipping the mom group. I watched "The View" and then braved the grocery store instead. But you know who I ran into at the grocery store? The only mom I met at the mom group, and you know what she said? "I didn't see you at mom group," in that tone of voice that insinuated I had skipped a high holy holiday. Determined to clear my mom rep, I apologized, but the truth was—I NEVER want to go to mom group again.

And then I felt like a worse mom for thinking that.

I grew up in a Presbyterian church where shame was subtle but present. It only took one visit to the mom group to realize that, when you become a mother, you convert directly to Catholicism. You take up daily penance and heaps of motherly guilt. Don't get me wrong: I love me some Catholics. My husband is Catholic, and all my extended family have rosaries. But now as a mother, I'm a new devotee with a fresh list of Hail Marys and Our Fathers to recite.

Ironically, I don't think anyone shamed Mother Mary. Now she was a MOTHER.

As far as I understand it, Jesus wasn't much about guilt either. Jesus was more about health care for the sick and helping the poor, all while sipping his homemade Merlot. He also adored his mother. So, this whole mom-guilt thing can't really stem from them; guilt wasn't present in the Bethlehem nativity set. No, it's us women who sling it, internalize it, and then hang it on each other like Christmas tree ornaments.

Why, dear ladies, do we do this to each other? Guilt is not a cute decoration. It's not festive. It makes our beautiful branches sag, and we already have enough sagging to worry about. Motherhood is a time to gather strength from our sisters, not drag each other down. We need to be our most compassionate. But do you know what we do instead? We compare, complain, and ultimately crush one another.

I didn't see YOU at the mom group.

If men were moms, they wouldn't throw guilt! They would fist-bump each other over a couple of PBR tallboys. They would skip the "Baby on Board" stickers and plaster a "Badass Dad Driver" decal instead. Every day would be a celebration of all their fatherhood accomplishments. Forget push presents— They would buy their own superdad rings.

Moms, pay attention. Maybe the men have something to teach us here (ahem). The men are not keeping a record of their shortcomings. (We do that for them, just like we do it for ourselves.) They are celebrating every victory, big or small. They are high-fiving their way to glory, proclaiming their fame. They are not taking note of who went to mom group, and neither should you.

◆◆◆◆◆

OCTOBER 29

Are you still tracking your baby feeds?
Yep. And poops. Every day.
I am too, but I now have a month of data. Now what do I do with it?
Maybe you can collage it? A cute at-home craft?
Ah yes, that beautiful excel sheet of shats. Should I also collage a picture of my daughter crossing her eyes? Because that's what she does when she shats.
Mine gives the fish mouth.
They can carpool to therapy together some day.
With their bowel movement charts.
The therapist will shake their head and blame it all on us.
Never chart the farts.

◆◆◆◆◆

OCTOBER 30

Ever since I gave birth, I have an incessant urge to clean, and I don't even like cleaning!
It's the nesting instinct.
I thought we already nested while pregnant?
It's all the same damn nest.
It's like I can smell dirt.
You actually can. The olfactory glands go on super drive in motherhood so we can ward off all toxic offenders.
Is that why I sport a travel-sized bottle of Scope whenever my husband wants to kiss?
For you?
No, for him silly. I swear I can smell anything like a mother.
You are a mother.
Well, I've become a cleaning machine. Nest tidying was my one task today.
How'd that go?
Baby girl had a blow out on the newly mopped floor.
They do that on purpose, you know. They see the mop coming and cross their legs until we are done.
It's just a regular fluid circus over here. There is no point in cleaning.

Every shirt I wear is drenched by noon. When people warned me I'd be doing mountains of laundry after birth, I assumed it was the baby's. How naive of me!

Seriously, I had visions of maternity leave being incessant amounts of free time to catch up on all those luxuries I never had space for.

Me too. I would wander through art museums with my baby perfectly Moby-wrapped to me and visit the sculpture gardens of Boston. I don't even have time to untie the frickin' Moby. Here I thought I'd really have time to see the city!

And expose my baby to culture. We would do music classes and yoga . . .

And postpartum Pilates!

What are we actually doing?

Bouncing and breastfeeding.

And ranting on texts.

Hey look, I can't even remember to zip up my own pants. Just stood up and the pants fell down.

At least you can button yours.

Apparently not.

◆◆◆◆◆

OCTOBER 31

Happy Halloween! Today I'm dressing up as Superhero Mother Multitasker. I will perform the death-defying feat of vacuuming with one hand while hand-pumping with the other.

I hope you are wearing a cape!

Always. Are you dressing up for Halloween?

Girl, I'm always dressed to impress in my sweatpants and scrunchies. P.S. I'm just now finishing breakfast. It's three o'clock.

Consider it a late brunch.

And I'm still sitting on the couch with steaming diapers on my boobs.

Girl, you are steam cleaning your child's favorite restaurant. Five points!

I need a star chart for these victories.

I'll send you one. Tape it to your fridge and put a big prize as the end goal.

Do buckets of candy count as a prize?

Of course they do. It's Halloween.

◆◆◆◆◆

I've decided to give mom groups another go, but this time, no large gatherings. I need a mellow group of ten women or less, so I don't lactate when all their babies cry. I also would love a mom group that's more activity-based. No offense but sitting in a church basement is not my ideal weekly outing, especially when all I do is sit home and nurse the rest of the week.

I've heard there's another mom group in town that touts themselves as the granola group. These are the ultra-organic moms, the attachment-based parents, the moms that gave birth while swimming with sea turtles.

I can jive with water births.

I put on my most flowing and floral dress, grab my softest cotton baby sling, and hike it to the park. Upon arrival, there are three women on blankets under giant oak trees, and two of their babies are fast asleep. Perfect—no leaky faucets this time around. The leader lady introduces herself and welcomes me to the picnic, where she's discussing baby carriers and passing around plates of French cheese. Oh, how European. And look how prepared I am for the baby carrier chat! Did you happen to see my soft cotton one made entirely of bamboo?

"I think you may have the carrier on upside down," the leader says.

"Oh, I prefer it upside down. I have a long torso," I lie. Besides, Isa's conked out inside that twisted pouch, sleeping up a storm. No one's adjusting anything.

The leader then shares the philosophy of the group, explaining that we sisters need to be there for each other during this precious time. I glance around at the other women in the circle. They look kind and caring, all around my age, all with boys. Isa could have her pick of the baby boyfriend litter, not that her father will ever let her date. I peer around again, glad my oversized black sunglasses let me inspect people without their knowledge. Strangely, everyone here seems laid back and without pretense. Within minutes, we are sharing birth stories and laughing over mom fails. The commitment level seems fluid. I doubt any of these women will shame me in the grocery store if I miss the group.

I like these women. They may be in my life for a while, and that promise feels very exciting. And just like that, I am officially in a mom group.

◆◆◆◆◆

NOVEMBER 1

On a different note, have you ever tried hubby-sucking?
I gave that up for lent.

It's a whole new level.

Nope, that leads to new humans.

Reverse it. And move locations.

Not following.

We had a medical emergency last night. I had tried EVERYTHING to clear my plugged duct, and there was only one thing left to do but call in reinforcements.

No!

Yes. Mateo removed the plugged duct.

No!

Thank God for single malt Scotch.

Stop it.

After a full glass, he went for it and voila!

I can't even.

My hero husband. It's healing now, still a little oozing . . .

Motherhood is a battlefield.

Normandy right here on my boobs.

I remember at our wedding I spent hours writing my vows. I need a whole separate vow list for parenting.

I vow to remove your plugged ducts, beloved wife of my heart. Now that sh*t is real.

In sickness or in health is much more family-friendly for the ceremony.

♦♦♦♦♦

NOVEMBER 2

Have you ever looked at the tags on your bibs?

Should I?

Mine say, "Machine wash. Tumble dry low. Light iron."

Who on earth is ironing bibs?

That's some serious cray-cray if you iron your bibs.

Jeff lived in Spain for a year in college. He STILL talks about his Spanish mom there with a twinkle in his eye. She ironed everything for him, even his underwear! I told him to be glad that fantasy was met already in his life.

Never again.

Wrinkled bibs all the way.

And then there's Enora's sleep sack. The tag says, "Do not throw in fire."

I mean, I almost threw mine in a fire last night when she wouldn't sleep at the monk hour.

What's the monk hour?

Those deeply spiritual twilight hours of 2–5 a.m., when the monks wake to pray. My daughter speaks in tongues during those hours.

She's a deeply divine baby, that Isa.

That's what I tell myself. At least she'll be the next Mother Theresa.

♦♦♦♦♦

Mindfulness takes on a new meaning when you become a mother. There is no option to not be present—your brain is so high on exhaustion, you can't think past the present moment. You breathe in desperation; you exhale coffee. You can't remember what happened a few minutes ago, nor can you predict what's coming. It's just sheer survival.

1–2–3-Exist.

It doesn't take long in Momlandia to realize that sleep deprivation is a legitimate version of torture. It's painful, but not like stub-your-toe pain. It's like a hangover without a cure, where coffee brings no relief, and you can't find your words or your hope or your hairbrush.

When I die and have my first face-to-face with God, I have a few more questions to unleash. First off, why do wars and cancer exist; those are obvious lead-ins. But then, I gotta sock it to Him straight: what in the universe was He thinking by making babies nocturnal? There is no evolutionary purpose to it. Yes, let's have women go through the hardest physical exertion of their life, where a human crawls out from the center of their souls, and then let's have them recover WITHOUT sleep.

Sleep—the only physical mechanism to promote healing. Sleep—the only mental prerequisite for sanity.

My husband and I sit together on the couch each night, after we lay Isa in her bassinet. Neither of us dares to look at the clock or ask, "What will we do next?" The thought of the night ahead terrifies us, knowing that every hour our darling daughter will morph into a hyena on her food quest. So, we hold each other in silence, aware that with each passing minute, we are closer to her hysterics.

It's hard to look forward to the night anymore. Night: that illustrious pleasure full of rest. Night: that time for cuddling and sweet slumber. Night was full of dreams and fluffy pillows and REM which took away wrinkles and gave me vitality.

Now nights mean interval training, where every ninety minutes, we awake to the alerting cries of our offspring, flail our arms to reach the baby bassinet, and unwrap the little one—all in utter darkness.

God, while I have you, if our young have to be nocturnal, why don't mothers have sonar? We have no way of navigating in pitch black, let alone for younglings that make David Letterman look like an early-rise. We can't nurture our babes in the land of black-out shades. Bats got the sonar superpower; why not us? Plus, bats raise their brood in colonies of thousands, so there's always an extra wing or ten to help. Next go-round at humans, please give us light detection devices, and while you are at it, the colony idea sounds good. Humans could use a few extra wings to help. Just saying. Amen.

◆◆◆◆◆

NOVEMBER 3

I'm reading a book my sister sent me called, "Twelve Hours Sleep by Twelve Weeks." I want to burn it.

Oh, sleep training! How funny. My mom group has banned that topic. It's too controversial among attachment parents.

Really? Everyone in Boston is sleep-training-their-child-to-Harvard already. I feel behind.

Ah, the two opposing coasts. In California, co-sleeping is all the rage, like they do in foreign countries.

You mean, like how Angelina did it?

Yes, I'm sure Brad helped perpetuate that co-sleep trend. How old is Enora now?

Eight weeks tomorrow.

Is she sleeping?

Not at all.

Wicked.

Maybe I'm a little late to the book.

Someone loaned us the Snoo. It's magic.

Is that the million-dollar bassinet that rocks them to sleep? I keep getting pop-up ads for it on my phone.

Worth every damn penny, particularly as a loaner. It has a sound and motion detector so when she stirs, it revs the white noise. It's saved my throat hours of shushing. There's also a built-in swaddle so she's kind of straight jacketed into the bed.

I always feel so bad when they are swaddled.

Me too. I know they supposedly love it, but it just reminds me of the snowy little brother in "The Christmas Story" who can't put his arms down.

Except now they can't put their arms up.

True confession: Before I had a baby, I thought shushing was mean.

Really?

I never understood why moms everywhere were just standing over their babies trying to shut them up. Now I UNDERSTAND.

Supposedly the womb is as loud as a 747 in there. The sounds remind them of the homeland.

Our bodies are freaking Mother Earth Space Stations.

How's Isa sleeping?

She eats every three hours round the clock, but the Snoo puts her right back to sleep.

Oooh, I need that.

You can rent one. Try Facebook Marketplace.

I'm thinking of second-handing everything at this point.

There's no point in buying new. Little girlfriend has a two-hundred-dollar newborn wardrobe that she wore for a week. I don't even pay fifty bucks for my boots!

You should. You deserve them.

My feet got fat in pregnancy. I'm still pretending they will shrink back to their original size.

I'm waiting for my whole body to shrink back to its original size.

Don't throw out your favorite jeans yet. We need an icon of hope.

◆◆◆◆◆

NOVEMBER 4

So . . . naps . . .

She will sleep if I hold her all day.

Enora too.

But then wake up as soon as I lay her down.

Our girls must be conspiring together.

So, can we talk about sleep training? I'm over Angelina.

Heck, yes. Supposedly we can start at six months. The idea is to lay them down drowsy and then provide reassurance until they learn self-soothing. I've heard it takes three days.

I'm not sure if I know how to self-soothe yet.

I'll teach you in three days.

Send ice cream, wine, and chocolate. Let the self-soothing begin.

◆◆◆◆◆

NOVEMBER 5

Speaking of soothing, have you tried a pacifier?

My mom bought her one, but it's sitting on the counter. She won't take it.

Neither will Enora.

I don't blame her. What woman wants to be silenced? It's very patriarchal to me. #metoo

Wow, I was much more simplistic. I'm more concerned with the future braces bill.

They will all need braces.

True. But isn't she still crying a lot? Wouldn't a pacifier help?

Don't ask. I know it's a blatant contradiction.

Everything in motherhood is.

♦♦♦♦♦

NOVEMBER 6

So, I read another sleep blog. They said we should stretch their daytime feeds from three to four hours.

Why's that?

So at night, they are used to longer stretches and won't wake constantly.

Seems logical. How do we stretch them?

Massive amounts of driving.

Again, supremely logical.

That's my new nap go-to. I got Enora to sleep for four hours today.

Did you drive for four hours?

Yup. I listened to lots of podcasts.

Brilliant!

Canada, here we come!

Increase the gas budget!

Gas = Sleep!

Sleep = Sanity!

Seriously, put on an audiobook. It's almost like a road trip vacation.

♦♦♦♦♦

NOVEMBER 7

I just spent two hours laying her down for a twenty-minute nap. If she wasn't so cute, I would have given up the ghost.

God makes them cute so we keep feeding them. Plus, "The Bump" blog says it all changes at eight weeks. We just crossed that mark.

Keep going.

Keep driving.

Do you know the new parent, on average, loses SIX months of sleep in the first year of a child's life? And for every night of sleep loss, it takes three days to fill the sleep debt?

So, we will be in debt until we're on Medicaid.

I also read this level of sleep deprivation is as good as driving drunk. Should we even be driving?

How else will we get the babies to sleep?

True. Always opt for the lesser of the two evils.

◆◆◆◆◆

New moms are hungry people. We feed humans from our pectorals. We pour milk from our hearts.

But not a single drive-through understands this.

If you are a new mom out running an errand, you will inevitably need lunch. And if you just can't stomach McDonald's, that leaves you only two options. Eat the yellow arches burger or be the bad mom who leaves her child in her car.

I confess: Today, I chose the bad mom option.

The bad-mom-lunch-dash is a ten-step program. Hi. I'm Jen. I confess I do the bad-mom-lunch-dash just like this:

1. *Drive baby around town until baby falls asleep. Even though you are polluting the world, promise to purchase renewable energy credits and save the globe in other ways. Keep driving until she passes out cold.*

2. *Ask Siri to find the nearest healthy lunch nearby.*

3. *Call Siri's vegan taco store suggestion and place your order.*

4. *Circle the vegan taco parking lot until you find the nearest spot OR illegally pull in the handicapped spot and put car flashers on.*

5. *Leave the car running so the baby thinks you are still driving.*

6. *Run into the store, rudely stare at the woman in front of you as she orders enough food to feed the local football team, each with their unique dietary restrictions. Doesn't she know I am a bad mom who has left my baby in the car? And even though that car is just steps from the cash register, can't she tell that I could be arrested at ANY moment? Lean into her shoulder, like creepy close, until she gets freaked out and stops ordering the special sauce for each tamale.*

7. *Order, swipe like your mama taught you, and dash back to the car to find your baby still sleeping.*

8. *Sigh in relief. Eat two bites of vegan taco from the driver's seat until the smell wakes baby, and baby smells you. Wave bye-bye to your lunch as her hunger trumps yours.*

9. *Put a nursing cover over you (this is your new napkin), and place baby underneath. Nurse left breast while eating taco with right hand. As you sit nursing, contemplate giving up nursing altogether to switch to formula.*

10. *Instead of switching to formula, vow to open a drive-through vegan taco joint, so no mom has to fear citizen's arrest over healthy tacos.*

11. *Covered in milk and tamale sauce, be proud of your activism dreams for all moms everywhere. It will distract you from the deeper question in life, like WHY IN THE WORLD did you bother wearing a white shirt to a taco joint?*

◆◆◆◆◆

NOVEMBER 8

We took Christmas card photos today.

Girl, it's only November. #SuperstarReindeer

The shoot took an hour. She protested the whole time in her Santa hat. Immediately after the shoot, she started uncontrollably giggling.

What a saucy little elf.

Saucy elf is a hungry elf. She cluster fed all day yesterday. She just wouldn't stop. I literally sat there eating tortilla chips and gelato the whole time, hoping the salt and sugar would magically convert to nutrients.

I've never been hungrier in my life.

Pregnancy cravings have nothing on breastfeeding. Oh, there she goes crying again.

Is she colicky?

I've yet to say that word. But she screams. A lot. On her belly. On her back. Pretty much all day. But if I don't say the word, she doesn't have colic. Because there's no cure for colic.

She sooo doesn't have colic.

Exactly. It's just a screaming phase that lasts every single day. The doctor said it should subside in a few weeks.

They say that about everything. Carrot-on-a-stick this momland is.

◆◆◆◆◆

NOVEMBER 9

Someone needs to write a "Kelly Mom" article on pacifier angst.

Girl, it's so real. I've spent sleepless nights over those damn nookies. To nub or not to nub . . .

I had no angst when she wouldn't take it. But I broke down and offered her the pacifier again today.

And?

She LOVES it.

Go with it, then!

But then I went to mom group and guess what? She's the only baby there with a pacifier, which obviously shouts from the rooftops that I can't soothe my baby without shoving earth-destroying plastic in her mouth.

There's so much Mom Shame.

In CAPITAL LETTERS. None of the other granola moms use a pacifier. Their boobs free-flow milk and honey like the Promised Land, and their babies suckle like wild bees. I'm Moses over here banging my head on a rock waiting for my letdowns.

Is your supply low? Wait, I take that back.

Don't say it.

Your supply is sooo not low. Back to the pacifier. I read that all the "vices" are just really effective tools, so rather than fear them, use them ALL.

Cookies, cakes, wine, pounds of dark chocolate.

Not OUR vices. For the babies.

They all seem like pretty good tools to me right now.

◆◆◆◆◆

NOVEMBER 10

I discovered my motherhood superpower. When Isa is in full baby meltdown in the car, suddenly I grow Go Go Gadget arms. I can magically find her mouth and shove in the pacifier, all from the front seat!

You are a rockstar! See, there's no pacifier shame in being a rockstar. You are Mademoiselle Pacifier Chauffeuse.

Oui, mais je ne parle pas français!

♦♦♦♦♦

NOVEMBER 11

The light is around the corner for you. Enora started napping three times a day exactly at two months old.

Daybreak is coming.

She's also going longer at night. We got a four-hour stretch in, and I didn't even have to drive to Mexico.

That's huge. I met a mom the other day whose baby is already sleeping through the night.

Did you punch her?

Almost. Then she started giving me advice like, "Do you have a bedtime routine? Do you play white noise and dim the lights? I massage, sing, and read him a bedtime story. As soon as we switched to the same bedtime routine, Billy started sleeping through the night."

Did you tell her Billy is a lump and has no personality and will likely have no friends by high school?

I withheld that detail. Didn't want to crush poor Billy's dreams.

Damn the mellow babies. So, here's my new sleep plan brought to you via London. Someone just gave me this British book about schedules, and I'm devouring every word.

Is it working?

So far. They are pretty detailed schedules. I can send you photos of the important pages if you want.

Yeah, the last few nights have been rough.

Maybe we should call Billy's mom. I bet she can fix everything.

Bite me.

That's Isa's job.

♦♦♦♦♦

After kids, you realize glamour has absolutely nothing to do with luring your husband; it has everything to do with your girlfriends. The spa and salon become a beacon of much-needed female prowess: an exotic oasis in the postpartum desert of frump. It's easy to get slumpy, and girlfriends are the perfect remedy for the trough.

As is the hairdresser. Today, I plan to celebrate motherhood by chopping all my hair off. Now, I've been gravely warned of the mom bob and swear it won't come to that, but Isa has an obsession with pulling my split ends, and I think she's trying to tell me something. Hence, the appointment with the hairdresser to beg for a banged non-Mom bob.

"I can't give you that," my very pregnant hairdresser says.

"Why not?"

"Because you have to blow dry your bangs. And I know you won't do that."

"I'm a mom now. I've changed. I have time to blow dry."

"You are lying. Moms have LESS time."

Fine," I pout. "You are right." And she is. If I cut bangs, I will look like the Addams family children, but darn it, I need a change. I dressed up in my cutest Target maternity jeans for this hairdresser date. I even put on mascara and graciously accepted the free glass of wine upon entry.

"What are my options?" I ask.

"How about a nice trim? I'll layer the front so your daughter can't pull it."

And with that, I leave with a nice trim . . . which immediately goes back into a ponytail. But it's not about the actual result, Ladies. It's about the illusion of change. Find freshness wherever you can.

◆◆◆◆◆

NOVEMBER 12

She's getting more independent. She stares at her mobile for a whole ten minutes these days.

That's enough time for a potty break and a coffee! I need a mobile! Where did you put it?

We have two. There's one over her crib, and I just got another to cart around with us wherever we go so she can stare at it.

SO MUCH STUFF.

She's obsessed with her mobile. Loves it more than her mom and dad.

Hey, I'll buy anything that occupies her for ten minutes. That's a luscious long time. I could invent things with that kind of free time.

Oh, I've submitted three patents already due to the mobile. It's magic.

♦♦♦♦♦

NOVEMBER 13

Do you know about hindmilk?
Hindwhat?
So apparently there's hindmilk and foremilk. The first few minutes a baby feeds, they get the foremilk at the front of the breast. We need them to get to the hindmilk, which is the fatty stuff in the back. That's the quality dairy.
So, I have a Brie cheese factory in my bosom?
Fundamentally, but you have to eat the cheap Kraft singles before you get to the fatty cream.
Is that why, when I pump, there's a layer of darker milk on the top?
Yes, so you should mix it.
I never mix Brie with American.
It's the European way.
Viva el queso.

♦♦♦♦♦

NOVEMBER 14

Have you heard of eat, play, sleep?
I read "Eat, Pray, Love."
This is similar, except there's no Italian delicacies or hot Balinese men.
Count me out, then.
Seriously, I've read the babes should eat, play, then sleep in cycles all throughout the day. So, you always separate nursing from naptime.
Isn't that the point of breastfeeding? To conk them out?
Yes, but not the point of sleep training. I've downloaded that whole British schedule. Feeds: 7 a.m., 10:45 a.m., 2 p.m., 5 p.m., 6 p.m., 10 p.m. Naps: 9–9:45 a.m., 12–2 p.m., 4:30–5 p.m.
That's WAY too many numbers.
It blurs my eyes too.
I've seen videos about this eat, play, sleep thing. But don't humans eat and then slip into a food coma?

It all seems so counter-intuitive. The only reason I'm using this schedule is because Enora does this one naturally. This way, I'm the superstar mom who placed her child on a schedule . . . that she already chose.

Good parenting tactic. Let's keep reading books that confirm what they are already doing.

Anything to bolster confidence.

Okay, my eyes have unblurred. I'm looking back at your schedule. What happens between 5 and 10 at night? There's a big gap there.

Alternating boobs and bath. 5—left boob. 5:30—bath time. 6—right boob. 7—sleep.

The evening window looks a little different over here.

What do you do?

Those are the YBB hours.

Your Best Breast?

Yoga Ball Bouncing. We bounce for hours. And I don't remember the last time we bathed her.

Not bathing is good too. Too much soap disrupts the system.

Too many numbers disrupt my system.

I'm madly reading everything I can to keep surviving. It's my method of sense making. Oh, I also read Isa's excessive crying should stop soon. It's her microbiome developing.

Do you ever reread our texts? Cluster feeding and microbiomes? This is a foreign language.

Baptism by fire, honey. Speaking of languages we didn't know existed, have you heard of the Dunstan baby language theory?

Wait, Isa is talking to me?

According to this Australian opera singer, Priscilla Dunstan, yes. This chick claims there are five distinct sounds that babies make. Each one communicates an important idea or need.

Such as world peace? And the reason for suffering?

Slightly smaller notions such as, "I have gas." I can't really make that sound out, but the "neh" sound is very clear for Enora.

What's "neh" mean?

It's baby speak for "I'm hungry." They "neh" when their little tongues hit the roofs of their mouths and they are trying to feed.

So "neh" is the hangry cry?

Yes. There are four other distinct cries, but you have to watch the videos. I'm finding it helpful though.

I'll give it a go. I'd love to know what the heck she's crying about.

◆◆◆◆◆

NOVEMBER 15

So, we ran into our Senator Elizabeth Warren last night at dinner. She held baby Enora for a photo-op.

The future is female!

Maybe our babies can be running mates one day!

I'm MORE impressed you went out to dinner last night.

Enora does really well out. I think we are too boring at home for her . . . Oh, I got the star chart you sent me! I taped that sucker to the fridge.

Awesome! What did you put as the prize?

A Coach purse if I cook dinner and feed the child for one month straight. The husband is ignoring the memo.

◆◆◆◆◆

NOVEMBER 16

I hate my whole wardrobe.

Sweetheart, I fit into nothing.

I thought getting a haircut would help, but now I hate my closet. I can't stand my maternity clothes anymore, but I can't squeeze into my former shirts. I'm in this weird beer-belly phase without the cute sorority poses.

We are shrinking. I have to believe it.

I'm not. It's official. Do you know what happened this week? I went to my chiropractor, and she told me I needed a belly wrap!

What's that?

A wrap for fat people. It's this strange corset apparatus to cinch me back together. She said my organs need to "find their way back home."

Damn. "ET phone home," right in our bellies.

I thought those bands were just for the Kardashians.

Nothing is off limits at this point.

I pouted and then ordered one. The gap between my stomach muscles is approaching Grand Canyon status. Then Jeff bought me a jump rope so I could work out from home.

Oh, poor guy. He doesn't know yet, does he?

That post-baby, mamas can't jump!

He sooo doesn't know about our leaky bladders. Well, you aren't alone. Do you know what came up in my Amazon recs today? "Expecting

More—The Fourth Trimester Workout and the Postnatal Slimdown" DVD series.

Isn't that waistline profiling?

Mom haters.

I do want to exercise though. I even ventured to a baby-and-me yoga class today. Does that count as a workout?

Hell, yeah! You burn fifty calories just lifting the car seat into the car.

Well, of course, everyone in the class looks fetching in yoga pants, and I still look prenatal.

Honey, you get two stars for even going.

It did feel sooo good to stretch.

How did Isa do?

Mid-lunge, baby girl had an up-the-backer. And then she started her protest cry. I had to take her outside—nothing could calm her highness down.

Radical woman, you birthed. What were the other babies doing?

Oh, you know. Singing moo cow songs and cooing. I downloaded the Dunstan baby language material, but she has no category for the anarchy cry. I think Isa hated the yoga playlist, honestly.

She's a revolutionary. Ain't gonna be caught in no moo-cow group-think process for this damsel!

Hey, I want my daughter to be a strong-willed, determined woman. I just need lots of rosé to survive in the meantime.

♦♦♦♦♦

NOVEMBER 17

Do you remember when the "unknown" used to be exciting? Like, "What cool thing is going to happen today?"

What a beautiful memory. That's all over, honey.

Yes! I now exit in fear when we venture out of the house. Did I bring enough diapers? Will she shart all over the restaurant? Will she shriek so loud that Child Protective Services will appear?

These little angel beasts are truly terrifying.

Strongest lungs I've ever heard. I remember, before I had kids, all of my mom friends would say, "Enjoy your freedom now!" I thought they meant big freedoms, like world travel and lazy weekends. You know what they actually meant? Tiny moments like running into the DMV without lugging a car seat.

I miss those DMV lounge days. I swear I'm becoming a hunch-back from the car seat lug.

So, we are shrinking and getting fatter. What a pretty combo.

Speaking of, I'm going on my first mom date on Monday. Pray for me.

Complete with child?

Yes, two moms and two children to the children's museum. Since Enora will clearly get so much out of the children's museum at three months old. But you know, it's located between MIT and Harvard Medical School, and all the moms here start the osmosis process pretty young.

I hope you buy her a college sweatshirt now.

I'll start with Ivy League bibs.

Well, my dear husband granted me a solo outing last night. I never made it past the bathroom, but that was a damn good bath.

Epic. I'm telling Mateo I need that kind of outing.

When I emerged, he was throwing her in the air reciting the times tables. They must have been going for a while because he was on table eight.

The difference between how parents bond astounds me. Wind down time for me includes books and lullabies. For Mateo, it includes wrestling and making fart sounds on her belly.

100 percent. Last night, I asked the hubs to mellow her out before we put her down. His activity of choice? Crawling CrossFit. He had her tummy scooting across the bed to build up her core. Poor girl was sweating up a storm to get the cupcake he put at the edge of the pillow!

I guess they need both energies.

True. Goodness knows, somebody should be building up their core right now.

How's the corset?

I wrapped it so tight I couldn't eat my own cupcake. So it was the cupcake or the corset. The pastry won.

◆◆◆◆◆

NOVEMBER 18

So . . . what's your sleep like these days?

She's becoming more and more solid with only a quick feed or two at night.

What about YOUR sleep?

I pass out like a dying lightbulb.

I'm so jealous. I don't think I've slept since the week I gave birth.

None of us have.

True, but it's more than that.

I thought the acupuncturist cleared you.
Briefly.
Is it insomnia?
Remember, we don't label things.
Oh right. You sooo don't have insomnia.
I'm also freezing all the time in bed, like night sweats but in an igloo. So maybe more like Arctic sweat hypothermia. I literally had a space heater on me and every blanket in the house last night. And I live in California!
#IcePrincessHormones
#AreABiotch
#WhenDoHormonesRegulateAgain?
#WhenDeathDoUsPart

♦♦♦♦♦

NOVEMBER 19

How long is your maternity leave?
I'm taking five months at seventy percent of my salary.
Wow. I'm taking four months at sixty percent.
Well, I'm using some "unpaid leave" and "vacation time" to stretch it out.
If men had babies, do you think they would code this experience as "unpaid" or "vacation?"
Are you kidding? They'd call it a SUPERHERO BONUS and give themselves an extra 25 Gs.
Let's do that, please.
But we get glamorous disability leave!
Yeah, men would not call this a disability. They would say they were Honorably Discharged from their career for a few months and hang medals from their chests. And then take the superhero bonus on top.
Could you imagine if they breastfed?
Oh, they would paste their faces on milk cartons like billboards.
If I opened my fridge to my husband's face on a carton, I can't even.
Oh, you wouldn't. You would be back at work getting paid what you're worth because you are a man.
Of course. The equalities are astounding.

♦♦♦♦♦

NOVEMBER 20

I heard the best marriage advice today. Let your husband solo watch your baby.

Like, leave the baby alone with him and trust everyone will make it out alive?

Yes. It's a practice of letting go of control for moms. And if the baby lives, your husband instantly becomes sexier to you because he cared for your young.

And if the baby doesn't live?

Everybody lives in this scenario. And then you get a much-deserved break.

But leaving the baby would require creating pages of substitute teacher plans. It's almost more work than it's worth.

No, you skip the sub plans and trust. That's the crucial part.

But what do you do?

Leave the house, pretend you are free, meet a girlfriend, and try not to talk about the baby. So when you return, you are missing the baby and you come home to a sexy husband.

Free time. I can wrap my head around that. Can't I make one little sub plan?

Nope. Trust.

Just what I'm good at.

♦♦♦♦♦

NOVEMBER 21

My milk is dying. My boobs are shrinking. My baby is going to starve!

Fenugreek. Mother's Milk tea. And power pumping.

My life has become one giant supplement list. More?

Do you want your child to starve? The Fenugreek really works. I also saw they sell lactation cookies now.

Coookiiiiies?

Milkmakers Lactation Cookie Bites.

Stop.

There's also the Boobie Bar. It's like an energy bar for your boobs.

I'm in the wrong business.

For realz, girl. Supposedly the stuff works.

Do you know my face got pudgier AFTER I gave birth? I lost fifteen pounds elsewhere and gained it in my cheeks.

Which set?

All of them. So, I got on the scale again.

Bad decision.

Only to track the baby's weight. I get on first, then pick her up, then do some ever-so-complicated subtraction.

My brain doesn't do that anymore.

My brain doesn't do most things. I guess "mom brain" is a legit reality.

We're just saving up our brain cells for tasks that matter most, like ensuring the human race survives.

Again, our paygrade is way too low.

◆◆◆◆◆

NOVEMBER 22

What sorts of toys are you using for brain development or stimulation? I need some ideas.

Um . . . a rattle?

Maybe I'm not so delinquent.

Instagram keeps targeting me with ads for toys that will advance her to college. Meanwhile, I keep turning on the Rachel Ray show hoping she will come cook for me.

Send her my way after she cooks for you! Oh, I've read that mirrors are good at this age.

Mirrors are SO not good at this age.

Not for you, honey. For the baby's mental stimulation. They like to look at themselves. It fires up their little neurons.

Oh right. Well, I threw all mine out, but I can gift them out of the trash to the baby.

◆◆◆◆◆

NOVEMBER 23

I went to the mommy yoga class again today.

How'd she do?

She shat everywhere again and cried. The two must be related.

Look at the bright side. You just made all those other moms feel like they are doing AMAZING.

True. They are now thinking, "At least my baby ain't like her baby."

Improving self-confidence in moms everywhere. Your reward in heaven will be great.

Many Coronas. I mean, crowns.

Easy to get those mixed up.

Coronas aren't gluten-free. They'd be wasted on me anyway.

♦♦♦♦♦

NOVEMBER 24

My milk supply is still dying. I think I'm gonna write a country song about it.

My milk is gone, my dog is lazy, and baby here makes me crazy.

Top 40, right there.

We could go gospel? God is great, God is good, please fill our sagging breasts with food.

Every priest will want to sing that one!

Seriously though, God will provide. Like manna in the desert, we only get enough food for the day.

But I want a whole freezer full of milk.

I don't think God sent freezers to the desert. Are you pumping after every feed?

Who has time for that? I still use only the hand pump, and nothing comes out after I feed. She eats it all.

Doesn't matter. It's still stimulating your body so it remembers to produce more milk.

I'm a crappy cow.

Have you tried formula?

We aren't saying that word. I'm determined to be my child's sole farm for at least the first year.

Of course not. We don't say many words. But if you need some, we rather liked this German organic one called Holle. We've only used once in an absolute emergency.

Leave it to the Germans to make an eco-formula.

Ze Deutsche! Most American ones are full of fillers.

So now I'll be ordering European meals for my two-month-old.

Pretty much. Maybe they can slip in a couple of bottles of Gewurztra-miner with your order.

♦♦♦♦♦

NOVEMBER 26

I figured out a new trick. If I bring the hand pump into the shower, I become a milk cafe! The hot water does the trick and voila! I have lots of milk again.

So practical.

Then I deep condition my hair while I'm pumping so I don't go bald.

You are like a multitasking Pantene commercial!

Isn't every mother? I think you actually spell the word mother m-u-l-t-i-t-a-s-k-e-r.

Motherhood seriously needs to be rebranded.

It's the most physically and cognitively challenging (and rewarding) project I've ever done.

I've been thinking about that recently, all these unseen tasks and skills of motherhood.

So much goes unseen.

Yes, and it takes huge mental bandwidth to track feeds and plan sched-ules and ensure safety and pack diaper bags. But then after you plan all that, you then have to go DO it all.

Very true. There's a big difference between THINKING about what the baby needs and DELIVERING what a child needs.

Correct. So, when Jeff takes her to the doctor, he's executing that task. But who made the doctor's appointment? Who thought of taking her temperature? Who Googled "safe baby fevers" to see if the doctor was an overkill? And who ran after the car to hand him her wipes?

You did, of course. Just like I do. And then you follow them in your car and go to the appointment as well, explaining everything to the doctor.

Exactly. But the executive planning part is a full-time job in itself.

That never ends or never gets credit. Do you really think our husbands stay up at night planning how to give the sex talk to our children one day?

Goodness sakes no, but that is the top of my list for night-time musings.

Exactly, while also planning the ten years that precede that terrifying talk.

So THAT executive job happens ON TOP OF the full-time job of baby care.

So, we are doing two full-time jobs?

You nailed it. We are a one-woman film set. We are the producers finding the baby props, the stage crew arranging the nursery, the janitors cleaning the kitchen, and the caterers making the meals.

All the heavy lifting.

But we are also the writer-directors planning the whole vision out. That's the hidden part, and it's an entire art in itself!

Pass me my Oscar, please!

Yes! In the film world, the highest honor is Best Director, after all. But in Momland, no one even acknowledges directing as a THING.

So true.

Instead, we call it "mom brain." Do you know what mom brain scientifically is?

It's a brain space invasion. Tumultus cerebrum.

Exactly. Our children literally crawled in between our ears and set up a tiny home with no plans of ever paying rent.

And then they do construction all day long in their tiny homes, as we mentally chase them, trying to prevent any harm.

No wonder we feel exhausted at the end of the day.

We're running ultra-marathons in our minds. And that's before we've even gotten out of bed!

And then, when we do get out of bed, the real race begins. Take, for example, the simple task of eating. I normally do all the grocery shopping, but my loving husband offered to grab some extras this week. I told him we mainly need avocados.

Let me guess. He came home with everything BUT avocados?

YES! And then he got mad I wasn't dancing in gratitude for the raisins he bought.

Let me guess again. You already have three bags of raisins.

Four! So now when he offers to shop, I not only have to survey the pantry for items we are low on, I need to write him a list, make sure he takes that list, and set reminders on his phone so he remembers to look at the list!

Group projects are so tiring. That's why I just do most of it.

I know, but we also need help. I waver between gratitude and complete annoyance. Take, for example again, last night's dishes. He rinsed a few and put them in the dishwasher. I'm very grateful for those few dishes.

What about the other dishes?

I did those. And unloaded the dishwasher. And ran the monthly dishwasher lemon cleanse. And locked the dishwasher shut so baby girl couldn't grab the knives from the silverware tray.

So, when my husband does one load of laundry and thinks he's shared the load . . .

He's shared part of the PHYSICAL load, but that's only a fraction of ALL of the loads.

As he pats himself on the back for his valor.

And wonders why we aren't patting him on the back too.

You're right. When you hear about the division of labor in marriage, it's always on the external physical tasks which, let's face it, are heavily skewed toward the moms. But no one talks about the executive tasks.

And when they do, they talk about it negatively, such as, "Stop being so bossy. Why are you so demanding!" Well, someone needs to direct the show.

You're right. The Oscars are the only place directing gets rewarded.

And men always win that category.

I hope our girls inherit a more just and aware world.

Where directing isn't viewed as bossy.

Well, I will say, since I'm trying to be fair, roles are not always gender specific. For example, I'm naturally a planner (which I enjoy) even more than many women I know, and Mateo is naturally the opposite.

True.

Similarly, Mateo is also better at other tasks. I just can't think of any right now . . . just kidding . . . sort of.

Look, I don't care if it's a female or male who wins Best Parenting Director, but someone has to at least ACKNOWLEDGE the award category.

Agreed. I'm happy to accept that award from you.

We gotta get props from our sisters, as nobody else is dishing them out.

Just wait until we go back to work. That's when the real lack of notoriety begins.

I can't, even. That imports a fourth tenant into the brain: baby, husband, self, work.

Can't there be a tenancy cap on this real estate?

Graciously, mom brains welcome anyone who knocks.

That's the motherly way.

✦✦✦✦✦

My dear friends made us a meal train for November, which means a few times a week, friends drop off dinner. I love this schedule—it's great motivation to pre-clean the house before they arrive, so my home only looks like half the hurricane that it is. Today, I picked up ice packs and nursing bras off the floor. I lit a candle and brushed my hair. I got out of my pajamas. My friends arrived. *I held up an adorable swaddled baby. She smiled. They awed. I pre-sented the world with what the world imagines motherhood to be—a freshly picked bouquet of cuddles.*

Damn, I needed that.

The meal train is the best therapy for new moms. It prevents them from eating cereal multiple times a day. It ensures nutrients are getting to the baby, as no first-time mother has time to bedazzle her dinners. And it lets her see friends, which reminds her of her civilized existence before baby.

If you know a new mom, bring her a meal. Hold her baby. And if her house looks clean, know that, while she did it just before you arrived as a gift for YOU, that scramble made her feel human again.

Meal trains are the most delicious treat.

◆◆◆◆◆

DECEMBER 1

Today, I Googled "baby songs that don't sound like Barney."

I just keep reminding myself that real music will once again grace our lives. Everything will one day be alright.

Funny you say that. Bob Marley popped up in the search!

Then every little thing's definitely gonna be alright.

I just can't embrace the gummy music. I refuse to succumb to "Baby Shark."

She's going to hear it somewhere, and then you'll be the mom who won't play "Baby Shark" for your child.

I'll take the heat.

Embrace the crap music.

I can't. It destroys my soul. Barney is banned forever, and I found an even worse one. It's called Tudy-Ta or something like that, and it has an animated dance music video. The lead cartoon singer looks like the white truck killer you should NEVER let your daughter near.

It's all terrifying, truly. Have you ever watched fairytales as an adult?

Horror films! Or what about lullabies? Rock-A-Bye Baby? "When the bough breaks, the cradle will fall!"

"And down will come baby, cradle and all?"

Now there's a bedtime winner.

Have you heard the Spanish lullaby, "Duérmete Niño?" It's about a wolf who comes to eat children in the dark.

Horrors. We went to South East Asia for our honeymoon. Malaysia has a bedtime song about dead baby chicks. It goes, "Five chicks, one chick dies, dying leaves four."

These make Chucky look like the Easter Bunny.

I'm never sleeping again. Oh wait, I already don't sleep.

♦♦♦♦♦

DECEMBER 3

Speaking of horror films, how's the sex life?

I told my husband the doctor STILL hasn't cleared me yet.

Genius.

The doctor did give me a pep talk though. She basically said lubricant needs to be my new best friend and not the hippy water-based stuff. The lady garage needs a quality oil change every time.

That's good advice. Wish we had known that sooner.

It's all so strange. The path that got us here seems so far from top-of-mind.

We schedule it now on the Google Calendar. And then we get too tired on the nights we've scheduled it.

Well, when you wake up every few hours, every second is precious. Last night we were so wrecked, we just got in bed and stared at each other. After a few minutes, I told him that was amazing.

Eye sex! Did you use protection?

I had my eye mask on, so I think we are covered.

♦♦♦♦♦

DECEMBER 5

Do you ever notice your texts with your husband have now become . . .

Hyperromantic?

Today we texted about diaper rash.

Oooh . . . Last night we texted about gas.

Sexy. I asked him if he'd pooped yet today. I meant to ask about the baby.

Not that you're not terribly interested in his bowels.

My whole life has become a B-grade medical show set entirely in the bathroom. Speaking of, does Mateo escape into the loo for hours on end? Or is this a my-husband thing?

Oh, I'm not sure what he does in there, but every escapade is at least thirty minutes.

It's a complete black hole. I opened the door the other night and Jeff was just scrolling through Reddit on his throne, as though he had all the time in the world!

Meanwhile, I nurse Enora from my throne. There's no time out experience over here.

None. But there are little windows where we can mobilize as a family in between her naps. I'm trying to get him to understand this. Jeff, we've got two hours before nap so let's go for a family hike. And then, as I load the car, he bolts to the restroom. A half hour later, our window is compromised, and baby girl is upset. No excursions today.

The dark vortex of the baño. It beckons the male species, like Sirens luring sailors off their course.

Seriously, I don't remember these issues pre-baby. To the contrary, I was glowing in love during pregnancy, and he could do no wrong. Now I have two husbands. My daytime husband (when not disappearing to the bathroom) is helpful. He does diaper duty. He folds onesies. He even washes dishes.

He's good at that physical load.

Yes, but once the sun goes down, I get nighttime husband. I want to KILL nighttime husband. He sleep talks, so he makes promises he doesn't remember. Last night, he slept yelled at me, claiming to change the baby, as she sat in my arms. We also can't hear each other over the white noise machine, so we whisper-scream at each other, half-deaf in the dark.

What if I want to kill my daytime husband too?

I hear there is gripe water for that.

He's off saving the world through his research each morning, while I brewed my morning coffee at 2 p.m. today. And then he comes home to a freshly washed baby and acts jealous that I got all this quality parenting time.

Look, add another star to the chart. YOU MADE COFFEE. Your Coach purse is coming.

I told him this morning that we need to start splitting the nights in half again. I don't care if I take the first half or second, but I can't continue like this. It's unsustainable, and I'm losing it.

Girl, I'm with you. Text me if you need to murder nighttime husband. I'm sure I'll be up counting sheep.

◆ ◆ ◆ ◆ ◆

DECEMBER 18

Enora has her first passport stamp. We made it to Argentina!
Massive amounts of star chart stars.

It was our Christmas gift to each other, visiting the extended fam. My husband's family is in LOVE with Enora. She's sleeping really well here too. I think she just needed some Buenos Aires in her life.

Don't we all? I'm drooling as I imagine you in exotic lands as I fold laundry. Cheap flights to nowhere were our pre-baby staple.

Oooh, it looks much more romantic than it is, traveling with a newborn. It's the same diaper bag but with none of your go-to gear. We are still pacing and bouncing and soothing her, just in a different hemisphere.

You mean, the baby doesn't magically pop open a Vogue magazine and take a vacation too?

Mateo said to tell you, "We are doing the same thing here as home, but we just paid 2G to get here." So now our child won't go to college, but at least she met her grandparents.

We are rolling in our saved dough then. Did you fly with frozen breast milk?

Yes, it was actually easy. You just have to declare it to the metal detector guards. But TSA does make you break down the stroller each time you go through security, even if she's sleeping.

I knew TSA worked for the dark side.

The whole experience was a bit of a racket, as we ended up tossing all the extra frozen milk after we landed in Argentina anyway.

Why?

She only nursed on the flight, so we didn't use any bottles. And apparently, once you defrost breast milk, it's only good for twenty-four hours. I literally threw out HOURS worth of pumping when we landed.

You can't get that life back.

Nope. Dead in the Argentine trash. Are you going home for the holidays?

We are flying to Seattle.

See, travel romance awaits!

Oh yes, going home to see the in-laws is super dreamy.

Grandparents are golden, no matter what.

Agreed. Just dreaming of foreign skies today.

We are in the foreign land of motherhood. That's exotic enough.

◆◆◆◆◆

DECEMBER 19

Have you heard of baby chiropractic? We tried it.

Yes, but even I am skeptical of that one. I don't know if they do it in Argentina, either.

They claim it can heal colic. And back aversions.

I didn't know she had a back aversion, and I thought we weren't saying the "c" word?

I'm over it. She has colic, and I'm desperate. She cries ALL day, but I realized the things she hates most are on her back: diaper changes, mat time, bassinets.

Did the chiro adjust her on the table?

No, she cradled her and just touched along her spine with her two fingers. Isa immediately pooped and passed out for a nap. I guess her occiput was out from birth.

Where is it now?

I think it's back in.

Good sleuthing. Look, she's almost twelve weeks! If we can survive the first three months, I've heard we will all keep living!

Yes, my doctor swears the screaming will subside at three months. That's just five days, three hours, and twenty-nine minutes away. Not that I'm counting.

We are crossing our fingers for you from Argentina! I admit, it's SO nice to be with family again. Even if they live across the world, they are a huge help. Christmas will be wonderful with your family too, I know it.

◆◆◆◆◆

DECEMBER 23

Feliz almost Navidad. How's Argentina?

The avocado toast trend made it here! Ironic, eh? And Enora is a champ. She's doing great with all the different foods and places we're going. She's also sleeping like a banshee. I think it's all a big joke on us, after all the hours I've spent trying to get her to nap at home.

I'm never napping her at home again. I'm just gonna take her out and when she gets tired, she can pass out on the fly. New goals, eh?

Turning over new leaves.

I also think I need to stop using my breastfeeding timer app as well, because I perpetually forget to turn it off. Yesterday, it said I breastfed for twenty-three hours.

Well, didn't you?
Definitely.
We are outgrowing the first stage of props.
Almost out of the fourth trimester!
TOTAL experts.
Isa just heard us say "expert" and vomited on me.
The battle is on, baby.
Did you get Enora anything for Christmas?
Um, we took her to see her grandparents.
Same here. Plus a wrapped-up shoebox.
They don't remember anyway, and kids go wild for cardboard.
That's what I'm telling myself.

♦♦♦♦♦

DECEMBER 31

Happy New Year! We are home and decided to do New Year's on the couch with movies, champagne, and both Japanese and Chinese takeout. Starting 2019 right!

Brilliant. We stayed up until New York had New Year's, then passed out on the couch out here on the West Coast. It was heaven.

What did Santa bring you?

Santa brought me jeggings—the best fashion for moms in belly bands.

Good Santa.

But Santa forgot to bring me a colic cure. Isa's three months and ONE WEEK. The doctor promised it would all be over by now.

Bad Santa! If it helps, we are drooling like a St. Bernard over here. Teeth are emerging. Isn't it too early for teeth?

Definitely. Don't you love these advanced genius things our daughters do?

I've heard that genius babies only sleep in Buenos Aires and colic exactly three months and one week.

MIT, here we come.

♦♦♦♦♦

JANUARY 1

New year. New goals. New electric breast pump.

I can send you my extra one . . . although I fried the chord in Argentina.

I've killed multiple hair dryers in foreign countries that way.

RIP, charger.

She refused the boob for the first time last night. It was a full-on-talk-to-the-hand move. That was her New Year's declaration. Hence, the need for an actual pump.

Enora hasn't been nursing well the last few days either. Maybe this is God's way of helping her get ready for being bottle-fed while I'm at work . . .

Work!

It's hard to believe I'll be back at work soon. I'm trying to negotiate a modified work schedule where I work remotely on Mondays and Fridays.

That would be amazing.

New year. New goals.

Working moms, here we come.

◆◆◆◆◆

Part of my New Year's resolution is to fix my stomach. Strangers still ask when the baby is due, and some don't even believe me when I say I'm POST-partum. For example, I gifted myself a reflexology massage over the holiday and the lovely Chinese masseuse refused my prone position.

"Baby," she said, flipping me on my back.

"Baby here," I said, pointing to the outside world.

"Baby hurt," she said, pointing to my stomach.

I didn't have the heart nor the Mandarin to explain to her that I've already had the baby. I know I still look rather pregnant, but the baby is out. After the massage, I showed her a picture of the baby on my phone. She hugged me and handed me a bottle of water.

I still don't think she believed that was my baby.

The first week of the new year, I plead with my physical therapist to fix me. An expert in healing diastasis recti (a fancy term for mom fat), she pushes her fingers deep into my belly blob. She shakes her head and writes some notes on her clipboard, only to return with her diagnosis: my stomach is now a sallow trampoline, like a well-worn toy my baby wrecked last summer. My elastic netting is broken.

Trampolines can be fixed, but it takes work to do so, and I've never been a gym rat. The PT hands me a pamphlet with pictures of stick-figure women doing sit-ups. If I become like them, I can heal my transverse abdominis, the corset muscles that cinch everything together. The stick figures also do way too many squats, "shhh" sounds, and leg lifts for my taste.

Isn't there a way to fix this WITHOUT stomach exercise?

"Well, you have a two-finger separation between your right and left stomach muscles. If we strengthen the transverse abdominis, it should slowly pull everything back together and then you won't have the gap."

"And then I won't look pregnant anymore?"

"And then your muscles will start to gather toward your body rather than falling out and away. Right now, those muscles are just surrendering to gravity."

"Among other things."

"All you have to do is twenty minutes of exercises five days a week."

Thanks. I'll be sure to add that to my whiteboard. Additional task for my non-existent spare time: trampoline repairman.

◆◆◆◆◆

JANUARY 5

In other fun breastfeeding news, I almost went to the ER yesterday because I had another plugged duct that was so painful, I couldn't clear it no matter what I tried. I steamed it. I bathed it. I soaked it. Then I repeatedly pin-pricked my nipple with a needle, and it finally opened up.

OMG. Did you just use the word needle and nipple together in one sentence?

Oh, many times. I keep needles nearby at all times.

I could never.

Oh, you have no idea. I have needles in the bathroom, needles on the kitchen counter, needles in my pumping bag for work.

Once again, you are my heroine. Here, I've been whining about my stomach.

I had no choice.

Maybe most heroines have no choice?

It doesn't really hurt. More like a pimple pop.

No man would EVER do this. I'm so sorry.

I don't know what's wrong with me, but I get plugs every week.

I guess we all have our cross to bear.

Your baby won't stop screaming.

And your boobs need Drano.

Let's just say I pardon my mother for all of her lifelong sins.

Oh, every damn one. How long are you planning to prick your boob with needles?

A year is the amended breastfeeding goal. I'd love to do two years, but if someone saw my needle collection, they might call Child Protective Services. How long are you planning on life as a colic mom?

OMG. I can't even. I'm calling in backup right now.

✦✦✦✦✦

JANUARY 6

Did you talk to the lactation consultant?

Yes. She said colic can be caused by food aversions passed through the breast milk. She told me to try an elimination diet.

What do you need to eliminate?

Peanuts, tree nuts, dairy, soy, wheat, fish, and eggs and then monitor if she screams less. She said the earliest I would see results is in seven days.

So, the anorexia diet? That would make me scream more.

Maybe I'll lose some baby weight? I'm trimming the trampoline, so to speak.

You'd have to. You'll basically be eating chicken and rice.

#GlutenFreeSoyFreeKungPaoToTameMyBaby

You are forgetting taste free.

Joy free. She also said to keep pumping, but Isa wants to be held all day. How in the world can I pump while holding my child?

Maybe that's why the Hindus have goddesses with twelve hands?

They knew about motherhood.

✦✦✦✦✦

JANUARY 8

How's the no-food diet?

I'm starving. I've boarded off the pantry to prevent me from entry.

Is it doing anything?

It's making me colicky! I'll tell you that. Did you ever hear from your job?

Yes! They approved my request! I can work from home on Mondays and Fridays!

Tackling the Ivy Leagues. SO HAPPY FOR YOU.

I don't know what I'd do without an amazing text buddy like you to get through this strange season.

Girlfriends are the most amazing gift in motherhood. This thread keeps me getting up in the morning.

You mean, your chicken and rice don't get give you something to live for?

◆◆◆◆◆

JANUARY 9

So, can we cut to the chase? Do we enjoy breastfeeding?

It's good for the babies!

But is it good for YOU?

It's not supposed to be, is it?

I don't know. It's supposed to be bonding, right?

Supposedly. Heck, I'm elimination dieting my way to every last drop.

What are your feeds actually like, though?

She screams on my boobs as I nurse and slaps them.

SO bonding.

I guess NOTHING about this experience is bonding. It's become more like a wrestling match that I refuse to quit.

I was trying to explain how challenging breastfeeding is to my community group at church, none of whom are parents, and I nearly hyperventilated. I could tell none of them got it.

I'm sure they didn't. They still live their life guided by enjoyment.

So, do we enjoy breastfeeding?

I can't answer that, because that would mean I'd have to ask it broadly, such as, "Am I enjoying this parenthood thing?"

There's no way to answer that. I've felt the best and worst of my life, so enjoyment seems like the wrong question. Maybe the question is, "Does nursing feel nurturing?"

I think I had visions of a sleepy bundle curled up next to me, gazing into my eyes, reflecting soul to soul.

That doesn't happen.

I swear it does for some people.

There's more romanticism around having babies than there is about falling in love. Neither looks much like the movies. Take, for example, my current situation. I'm sitting in the car in snowy weather waiting for Enora to finish her nap. I ran as many errands as I could think of . . . got gas, went to Target . . . and now I'm just in the front seat texting you.

You have the heat on, right?

Heat's on.

If you bring the car seat in the house, what happens?

It's hit or miss if she will wake up. It's not worth it if she wakes.

Bonding time, winter edition.

♦♦♦♦♦

JANUARY 10

I had an epiphany.

What's that?

Remember before kids we would go out to a movie and the next day a friend would ask, "Did you enjoy it?" And sometimes I'd say, "It was fabulous!" and other times I'd say, "It was nice, but not a film I need to watch again."

Yes . . .

Do you remember those days of OPTIONS where even things you fully enjoyed, you could say, "I don't need to do that again?"

Yes . . .

We don't live in that world anymore! Now, whether you love it or hate it or feel ambivalent about it, you still HAVE TO DO IT! Every other hour.

Very true. Before parenting, I'd shape my days based on what I enjoyed doing. And yes, I adore many aspects of motherhood, but there's so much about parenting that I simply don't want to do, but it freaking HAS to get done.

So we now live in the world of must-get-dones. And while some of those must-get-dones bring deep fulfillment, some are just FREAKING hard.

It has to get easier. I think this newborn stage is just the most intense.

So back to the movies. Exhibit A: Jeff got me a movie theatre gift card for Christmas.

What's that?

Exactly. Pre-baby, that would be a normal Friday night. Now, that's a far-off goal I'll feel bad enjoying. My mom comes back at the end of February so maybe we can attempt a date then. Although her generation never had the luxury, and she'll likely wonder why I need to leave my baby to go see a film.

There has to be a middle ground. Date nights are healthy.

Many things are healthy for moms, but it often involves time AWAY from baby—a conundrum in and of itself.

Wait until we go back to work. That's where the real battleground of impossible standards begins.

Work like you don't have kids. Mother like you don't have a job.

Feel like you are failing both.

Thank God we aren't there yet.

♦ ♦ ♦ ♦ ♦

JANUARY 11

My latest self-care obsession? That spark joy chick who tidies your house and throws out all your junk.

OMG. I tried watching that show, and I puked a little in my mouth when she talked about infusing love into your folded undies. I had to turn her off.

Ignore her folding part. I'm having visions that if I watch enough episodes, my house will become clean through osmosis.

That's a fabulous fantasy. Maybe I should give the show a second chance.

She has this part about sentimental items that's helpful. I realized that I don't have a single sentimental photo in my home. Shouldn't I have photos of Isa all around by now?

I just finished my wedding album! I forced myself to finish it before Enora was born because I knew I'd never do it otherwise. Three years late but better late than never. Have you taken any coordinated outfit family photos yet?

Are you kidding? Not until my trampoline heals will I pose for a full body shot.

You always make me feel better.

I also missed the cement footprint moment. Her feet are giant now, and she's going to grow up and ask where her cement footprint ornament is!

I don't think they cement children's feet, honey. I think it's more like playdough.

Whatever. Someone gave us a "My First Christmas" ornament before the holidays. You stick their little feet in white paint and press it on the bulb. Does it matter if we make the ornament in January?

I won't tell.

I'll only press part of her foot into it; that way it'll look smaller and more realistic.

Work smarter, not harder.

Will I ever not feel behind?

Ask the spark joy chick. Maybe if we throw out our wardrobes, life will become more spacious.

◆◆◆◆◆

JANUARY 12

So, can we talk about brain development?

Ours or the babies?

My brain has no growth right now, but I just read that babies have these times of intense brain change, and this Wonder Weeks app can predict those days for us.

Yes, we have that app. You enter your child's birthdate, and it forecasts which weeks she'll undergo rapid neurological development. Those are the brain "leaps."

Is it accurate?

Scarily so. It's been spot on for us.

What's a leap like?

Hell.

So I catch on fire?

Basically. It's a full fussfest. Fussy eating. Fussy sleeping. Fussy everything. Solid eternal torment.

Bring your own pitchfork! Why in heaven didn't I know about this before? Maybe she's always in a leap!

Or we just have genius children, whose brains have already surpassed Einstein's.

Obviously.

The app does make me feel less crazy knowing her crankiness is SUPPOSED to happen. I get a text message warning from the app saying, "The leap is coming." On those days, I double down.

Because she will act like a baby psycho.

Precisely. And make us mom psychos.

This is life changing.

Turn on the reminders. It's seriously so helpful. We are both in Leap Four, and it says that as babies approach this leap, they often refuse the breast. It's common for mothers to feel rejected and confused and think it's time to wean the baby. The app explains that, on the contrary, you should not wean the baby but rather keep breastfeeding, as the rejection is only temporary.

I think the answer to everything is, "Don't wean the baby."

I think we are told imaginary finish lines, so we don't quit. And when we get there, we realize there's another finish line.

If you can make it through labor, then the work is done!

If you can make it through the fourth trimester, then you will be home free.

If you can make it through breastfeeding, your child will get immunities.

If you can get them to college, they won't live in your house forever.

If you can send them to college, you'll be broke for the rest of your life.

And if you make it through this leap, then they will have mastered the "world of events." They will comprehend series and transitions.

Transition this. Do you ever roll your eyes at yourself as you type? And then still believe EVERY SINGLE WORD?

Every damn day.

I shouldn't make fun, as I haven't eaten real food in weeks.

Is the diet working?

It worked for a minute. She's still a crying mess, but now I'm scared to start eating foods with flavor again, as what if it makes it worse? What if Level 8 crying is an improvement and if I eat food, it will go to Level 10?

I'm telling you, it's the Leap. Hold tight.

◆◆◆◆◆

JANUARY 15

So, I'm sending you a pic of my nursing bra because it's too naughty not to share.

Is it black with slits over your nipples, and do two bottles hang off from you?

How did you know?

I have the same bra! Mateo calls it my BDSM top.

Spicey. All we need are whips to complete the outfit.

Just use the breast pump tubes. Isn't that what they are for?

◆◆◆◆◆

JANUARY 16

So, have you tried it?

Tried what?

Your breastmilk.

No. Am I missing out?

It's remarkably sweet. I tried a drop the other day from Isa's bottle.

I'll be sure to offer some to the husband with his scotch. It can be the BM White Russian.

BDSM White Russian.

Be sure to wear your nursing bra when you serve it.

Every man's fantasy.

◆◆◆◆◆

JANUARY 19

Every day my milk supply gets worse. What is wrong with me?

Girlfriend, I just had a breakdown over my supply. Literally, I asked Jeff to hold me and tell me I'm not a failure if I start supplementing with formula. Who does THAT?

This breastfeeding stuff runs so deep.

It cuts to profound levels of insufficiency.

As a woman, I should know how to feed my child.

As attachment parents, we should breastfeed until college.

I spent twenty minutes in front of my freezer yesterday, debating how much frozen milk to thaw for our family flight to Seattle. Because once it's defrosted you have to use it, as you know, and I was petrified I'd run out of food. I put the bag in the freezer then took it out again twice. I was in full paralysis over six ounces of milk!

It's because we don't have a lot to spare! We are living pump session to pump session with this impending deadline of returning to work.

I thought I would have a freezer full of backup milk by now. I have ONE solo bag for emergencies.

Me too. One bag. That means no leaving her or else she'll starve.

We are gonna go buy some more formula.

Us too. What's the name of the formula you used again before your milk came in?

Holle from Germany. I'll resend you the link. Don't feel guilty if you end up needing to supplement with formula. Generations of Brits and French are formula-fed and look at how well their countries are doing!

I'm not ready to wave the white flag yet, but I need some in the house.

There's something to be said for keeping your sanity and THAT is the gift to your child.

Are you calling me insane?

We all have our edges.

It's hard to choose sanity when everyone seems to effortlessly feed their child with boobs that flow like the Euphrates.

Okay, I found some Holle on Facebook Marketplace. Gonna go pick it up tonight.

(extended pause)

But are you going to USE it?

I just want it in the house for peace of mind.

I know. Emergency ordering formula from Germany is kind of a process.

(extended pause)

You know, I read the best time to pump is between 1 and 4 a.m. as that's when we produce the most prolactin. The prolactin tells the brain to produce more milk.

That could work . . . No wait, that will not work. I've gotta draw the line somewhere.

I'm setting my alarm. We've got this.

Why do we keep saying that?

Because maybe it's true if we keep saying it.

◆◆◆◆◆

JANUARY 28

Well, the goat milk formula arrived from Europe, and I've shelved it for safekeeping. I'm eating Fenugreek by the pound, and I found a recipe for wheat/dairy/soy/egg/fish/nut-free lactation cookies that supposedly can boost my supply. I don't usually drink beer, but I'm now sipping brewer's yeast by the gallon, along with flax and blessed thistle and every galactagogue possible in hopes the galaxies align for milk.

In the Bible, there's the story where the crowd runs out of food, and Jesus miraculously makes oodles of grub out of some fish and bread. I need that kind of milk miracle. I have one bag of breast milk left, and I'm stepping out in faith that my body will become a raging white river, so I can stack that freezer full of glorious Lansinoh ziplocks.

My daughter is four months old. I desperately want to exclusively breast-feed for a year, and I've never bowed out of any goal in my life. Sweet Jesus, pass the bread and fish. Let this mama make milk!

♦♦♦♦♦

FEBRUARY 2

I started work.

God bless you. How's it going?

Remember how I asked to work from home twice a week? Today was my first day attempting that.

Do you love it?

Well, Enora chose today to start another nursing strike, so I've been pumping and bottle feeding. She also chose today for a nap strike, so I carried her all day. Then she threw up twice, but she kindly waited until I changed my outfit for the second vomit.

Sounds like the warm work welcome you've always dreamed of.

Chocolates and roses from my daughter.

You survived day one! What about the other days when you go to the office? What are you doing for childcare?

We found this daycare we loved.

Great.

But then a baby died there.

Oh my goodness, that's horrifying.

Needless to say, we didn't enroll.

I hope not!

We then found this woman/angel from our church for $15 an hour. She brings her six-month-old over with her, so Enora has her first boyfriend.

That's heaven sent. Well, it will get better. It has to. This is only day one.

That's what I keep telling myself. The sun will come out.

Tomorrow.

Like all things in parenthood. Gotta go. She's SCREAMING again.

♦♦♦♦♦

Colic has a strange way of flip-flopping you. Some days, I'm convinced my child is existentially revolting against all of life's pain. The world is an over-whelming place and someone needs to cry about it, so God chose my baby to be the world's weeper. Other days, I'm sure she's just a whiny brat, protesting for no reason at all. Most days, I'm convinced my child's gut is swollen in agony, and there's no Pepto Bismol to help. That's what colic does to the brain. I alternate between, "My child is in pain," to "My child needs to learn gratitude and shut it." I also alternate between deep compassion and wanting to drop-kick her.

Today, I'm in the PAIN camp. I'm also in the desperation camp. I have two weeks left until I start work and leave my chatty cherub with a nanny, so I must sequester a remedy. I can't imagine leaving my screaming infant with an unsuspecting Good Samaritan, particularly when that Good Samaritan is a mom from my mom group. I need her not to quit on day one. In sheer desperation, I cart myself to the homeopath, hoping some foreign herbs and ancient tinctures will heal my child's mortal soul.

At the homeopath's office, I hand her my list of concerns, and whisper, "Help me."

Help Me, Please

Baby girl hates being on her back. Bloody murder all the way.
She screams during her daily feeds.
She screams after her daily feeds.
She screams after every nap.
She wakes all night long in tears.
She has eczema on her cheeks and chest.
She's either constipated or blowing out.
She has a tortured cry that builds throughout the day. By evenings, she's inconsolable and purple. NOTHING works.

The doctor looks at me and peers at my baby, who, of course, is statue silent in my arms. "Please believe me," I say. "I'm not crazy. I need you to trust what I'm saying."

A few hundred dollars and some tinctures later, I leave with a bag of holistic remedies. I can't pronounce any of them—a sure sign they will work—but at least I feel organically proactive. Any movement forward helps. Baby steps out of colic.

◆◆◆◆◆

FEBRUARY 4

We are now on multiple distillates from the homeopath. It's February. There's no end in sight. My new strategy is to give up all hope. With low expectations, maybe one day I'll be surprised at her happiness.

Do you think it's a food allergy?

I've been on the no-allergens diet for a month. I'm hardly eating any-thing, and she still turns purple in fits. I can't take it much longer. I'm wearing soundproof headphones for sanity today.

Has the diet helped?

Nope. And I've had no weight loss on it either.

So, no perks at all. I'm hungry all the time without being on a diet.

I'm starving and still don't fit in my jeans. Am I allowed to admit I'm jealous of mellow babies?

Remember, they will be duds in life.

What about moms who fit in their pre-baby clothes?

I'll punch them all for you.

♦♦♦♦♦

FEBRUARY 5

So, these were my texts with my husband today:

Her colic will never end.

I thought it already ended?

Don't you notice? That was just one day she was happy. Oh wait, you were at work.

Maybe it's not colic, and she is screaming for real reasons.

Very true, but why are you siding with her?

We are her parents. It's our job to understand what she needs.

But I need you to understand me first. Last week, she was hurting in pain. Today, she's angry for nothing.

You are getting angry for nothing.

Nevermind.

♦♦♦♦♦

Dear God,

It's been a while since my last confession. This time, I almost punched out the yoga teacher.

If you haven't noticed, I've become a little frazzled. My mother arrived at our house this week from the East Coast, and she urged me to take the afternoon for myself, sensing my growing angst. I thought a yoga class would be a healthy option, the sweatier the better to purge out the cortisol eroding my veins.

But I wanted the sweat to be mine.

I'd been dreaming of a real workout class for months—one where it was just me on the mat. I was dying for personal space. In retrospect, I should have known to leave when I saw an overly packed class, but this was my sole opportunity for rehab. Instead, I took the last floor space near the teacher. I closed my eyes. I centered. And then I felt someone brush past my leg.

I opened my eyes to see the yoga teacher, already sweaty from the 110-degree room, pacing the floor. He was not a stationary leader. In fact, he never stayed on his mat at all; he paced left and right. I kept trying to focus, but it's hard when every sun salutation, sweaty-smelly-yoga-guru walks OVER you. If that wasn't enough, SSYG (sweaty-smelly-yoga-guru) had a medical-grade perspiration issue. He didn't just drip. He was a walking sprinkler system. By Krishna Das song four, I was drenched with his dew.

I tried to Om. I tried to breathe. But I couldn't take it. I have enough fluids of my own to deal with; I don't need yours, and this in the ONE HOUR I have to feel cleansed. I curled up in child's pose, hoping to protect my face, but then, he passed and kerplunk! SSYG dripped right in my open water bottle. That was it. I had no option but to peacefully protest in a walkout.

"Are you okay, ma'am?" the front desk yogi asked, seeing me march out of class.

While I contemplated practicing non-violence, my mouth became an uncontrollable volcano. "No, I'm not okay. I'm a new Mom. I don't get out much. I spent a month's worth of diapers in cash to attend this yoga class, designed to RELEASE my stress, and do you see me now? I'm dripping wet and worse!"

"I'm sorry, Ma'am," she said. "It IS hot yoga, after all."

"I've done hot yoga for years. I spend my days covered in spit-up. I did not pay to have your teacher drench me with his toxins. See my wet towel? My water bottle? That's him alright!"

The woman behind the desk stared back at me, and instead of pausing like a normal person would, I just continued. "I know this is crazy, and I sound crazy, but moms are crazy people and is it too much to ask to have a non-drip teacher? I don't mind crowded classes, but at least give me the personal space of my own yoga mat!"

"What's your last name, Ma'am? I'll write a note on your account."

I gave her my name and bolted for the door, trying to make it to my car before a full tearfest. But then, God, I panicked more. She wants to write a note on my account? What does that note even say? "Crazy Ass Mom—do not admit. If you admit, do not drip!"

Speaking of dripping, I then had a letdown and sh*t got real.

God, I know you won't give me more than I can handle, but your expectations of me are WAY too high right now. I'm not qualified for this job. I know some people have true, sick children, and all I have is a child in perpetual colic, but I'm not coping well! I wasn't invented to hang out with screamers!

Look at me, God! I've become an angry person. Isa's anger makes me angry—the sound of her blood-curdling screams echo straight into my bones and rot. And then I'm a rotten mom. I just want to place her in a field and whisper, "Life is good. There is sun. There are flowers. You are fed and clean. And life doesn't get any easier kid, so shut it! One day, you will go to hot yoga and a teacher will sweat on you, and then you can cry yourself a river!"

Maybe I need to lay down in a field and shut it—I know she's a gift, but we are just not on the same wavelength right now, and it's destroying my soul.

Every mother I know is madly in love with her children, and I'm not sure mine even likes me. She won't settle in my arms, and she riots in my face. This was supposed to be my bonding leave. I'm supposed to be an attachment parent, and I've yet to attach to my child. In all your spare time solving world hunger, can you throw a tiny bone my way? I promise to give to the Salvation Army in return and fund research for colicky kids everywhere. Until then . . .

Love, Jen

◆◆◆◆◆

The next morning, the clouds rolled away. I'm not sure if it was the desperate prayers or the homeopath's tinctures or simply the breakthrough of time. But sweet Jesus, Isa woke up happy. She's smiling. She's giggling. The house was eerily quiet ALL DAY LONG.

Life seemed possible again.

Over the next few days, I dust off myself from the battlefield. I put on my big girl pants, sans zipper of course, and find some return-to-work clothes. My maternity leave was far from the bliss I was marketed, but it was our story, and that story is evolving.

In my final days off, I ring my therapist again. My pediatrician basically mandated me there, mentioning that post-colic moms are often traumatized from their mothering experience. I was. I am. At the therapist's office, I tell her I failed at my child's most important time period. All I wanted was yummy cuddles, and all my daughter did was wail. She reminds me that attachment is a life-long process of repairs and returns to each other.

She reminds me I haven't missed my chance. There's always time to spread more love, to bond. I weep in her chair like a baby, releasing the months of screams I shouldered for my daughter. She holds space for me; I held space for Isa. Everybody needs a little space held for them. That's how everybody makes it out alive.

I begin to feel normal again. The night before I return to work, I write my nanny a confession. To be fair, it's more of a dissertation of my mothering struggles. I want her to know the strong child she's signed up for. The nanny is also a fellow mom in my mom group, so she's seen me in the thick of it.

"I've never met a baby I didn't like," she tells me. "Parents, on the other hand, I've met a few of those." I knew then she was the right woman to watch my daughter. And I'll try not to be that parent, promise.

Baby steps.

◆◆◆◆◆

FEBRUARY 11

Day one work goals: apply lipstick, wave hello to everyone and tell them how amazing maternity leave was, have an honest cry with a coworker, and pump. I've now completed all my work goals, and it's only 10 a.m.

You are a rockstar. I'm sending you champagne RIGHT NOW.

What's your work goal today?

To find a therapist.

Ooh, I just started seeing mine again. What's yours for? Work? Baby? Husband?

All of the above. I just feel disconnected and overwhelmed. I just ordered a book called, "How Not to Kill Your Husband After You Have His Baby."

Step one. Hide all knives . . .

Seriously. There's just a lot on my plate and the plate feels bigger and bigger each day. The allure of going back to work has worn off, and I'm just buried.

I think our true work is just unfolding. I just don't know what it is, and I'm not sure how trained I am for it. I don't know how to be a great mother, let alone a great working mother.

No one does. Everyone is just faking it and barely treading water.

While hanging over us is a giant SHOULD. We should know what we are doing.

It's all so unnatural. I'm attached to a milking machine right now at the office, and my child is at home with a woman I met a few months ago.

I know. My husband dropped off Isa for her first day today too.

I don't think I could be a stay-at-home mom. But I'm not sure I can be a working mother either. So now what do I do with my life?

I'm only a few hours in, and I feel you. Do you think our husbands felt this?

Um, Mateo went back to the lab the day after Enora was born. He didn't even take a paternity leave.

Neither did Jeff. He worked from home for a week and then back to life as usual.

The male/female divide again shocks me. Even though we have adoring, doting dads, it's still amazing how different the work/life balance is for women and men.

Well, they aren't plugged into milking machines on the job. It doesn't affect their biology. Our bodies are physically wired to our babies.

For better or worse, until death do us part.

This is love.

♦♦♦♦♦

FEBRUARY 12

So, the nanny said Isa was an absolute angel yesterday.

Prepare for that. Your child will be her very best self with others, and then you'll wonder what all the fuss was about the last five months. But trust me, it was real.

It's so strange. It's like she's watching a different child! Or maybe I was just doing it all wrong.

Does your nanny have a child?

Yes, a little girl Isa's age.

Same with us. I think that's the trick. The babies perform for the other babies.

Oh, shoot. Maybe I should have gone the sibling route.

There's still time.

♦♦♦♦♦

FEBRUARY 13

So, tomorrow is Valentine's Day. I should probably wash my hair again, right?

Dry shampoo baby.

I bought some more yesterday.

It's magic. It should only be marketed to moms.

And then they would upcharge us 50%.

And we would still buy it in spades.

Very true. Now WHERE did I put the lovely bottle?

Check the fridge. That's where I put things when I'm comatose.

Voila! How did you know?

Because that's where working moms park. You're either storing breast milk or raiding the fridge. Either way, you are THERE. Anything lost is found in the fridge.

Amazing grace.

◆◆◆◆◆

FEBRUARY 14

Happy Valentine's! In the spirit of romance, I'm back to hating nighttime husband. Yesterday, Jeff was a saint. Changed all diapers, bathed the baby. Then in the middle of the night, I fed Isa and handed her to him to change her. That's the arrangement. I feed. He changes. So he says, "Thank you," and just lays there. So then I get up to change her and he yells, "No, no, I've got her" and falls back asleep. So I change her and put her back to sleep, and then he pulls her out of the bassinet, and says, "She wants to sleep in bed with us!" So there we are at 3 a.m. in a philosophical argument about co-sleeping until we all pass out. By morning, it's all phantom, and we kiss and go to work.

OMG, YES. Half the time I'm amazed at how sweet my husband is and the other half, I'm scared out of my mind at his inventive ideas.

Do you just pretend all middle-of-the-night rifts don't happen?

Yes, particularly on Valentine's. Salvage any sparks you've got.

◆◆◆◆◆

FEBRUARY 15

I put my shirt on backward after pumping at work today. Then I went into a meeting. It was awesome.

Stop terrifying me. I did that sh*t before babies. I have no hope.

My milk perked up for a few days when I started using a hospital-grade pump at work. It makes a big difference.

I just put in a request to my insurance for a hospital-grade one.

What did they say?

It's in the mail! And it even came with accessories. I could choose either the flower transport satchel or the ice pack.

Go with the transport bag. You will be carting those bottles everywhere with you.

♦ ♦ ♦ ♦ ♦

FEBRUARY 18

My new pump arrived. I was so excited, I forgot to bring all the parts to work.

You can always hand express.

Hand pump baby. Never leave home without it.

You and your hand pump.

I've actually never used an electric pump until work this week. Last time was in the hospital on day one.

Mazel Tov! Have you tried that new lactation cookie recipe I sent you? I made a big batch and froze half of them.

I'm eating them right now actually. I got an ounce more from these magic cookies.

The brewer's yeast is the key ingredient for milk production.

And the chocolate chips are the key ingredient for sanity.

Do you remember when we were in college and thought, "I can't wait to change the world!" And now, nearly forty and mothering, all we think is, "Please, God, let us remember the lactation cookies in my work bag."

Is this us living our best lives?

Define BEST?

Wow, let's go existential. I've got a twenty-minute date with the hand pump, so let's go there. So . . . I was never that girl desperate to be a mother.

Me neither.

I met my husband, though, and was, dare I say, inspired to have a child with him.

Me too.

And while it's carved a place in my heart that I didn't think possible, I thought I'd feel a deeper level of fulfillment by now.

Sitting at work attached to your pump?

Well, some women wait their whole lives for babies or can't have kids at all, and here I am, back to work, covered in milk splatters.

I read this today, maybe it will help us. It's a quote by Rachel Cusk. She says, "Motherhood is a sort of wilderness through which each woman hacks her way, part martyr, part pioneer; a turn of events from which some women derive feelings of heroism while others experience a sense of exile from the life they knew."

Boom, that's good. That's exactly it. I feel like a pioneer in exile, trying to get back to the motherland.

Except now we are the motherland. We are learning to come home to ourselves.

It's a slow evolution, this motherhood. Thanks for leaving the light on for me.

♦♦♦♦♦

When you are a mom, you become proud of small accomplishments, accomplishments that no one else would even recognize as an accomplishment, like putting your shirt on forwards. For such feats, you get to reward yourself with numerous galactagogue treats.

This week's feat: mastering the new electric pump. My first few attempts were slightly less than oil-smooth. I sat down on the rocker. I stared at the nursery pictures on the walls. I double-checked the blinds and then double checked them again, convinced some schoolchildren might spot me. I wondered how my career had led to this. Then, after attaching all the parts, I realized my bottles were in my office, so time to reclothe and start the process afresh.

Now, I've got it down to a science. I stop in the work kitchen to microwave the gel pads. I grab that lactation cookie. I swap clothes into my nursing bra and insert warm gel pads. I turn on the pump to automated settings. I place my work laptop on my knees, so I can answer emails in real time. I remove said laptop before detaching pump, so I don't spill liquids on technology. Then, it's time to reclothe, splash water on my cheeks, and put my game face on for another three hours.

My day is now divided into these three-hour chunks. Work, pump, refresh. Work, pump, refresh. After work, it's now mother, nurse, cook, then mother, nurse, clean. Somewhere in there is sleep, but since I'm behind on that, why not feel behind on everything else?

It's okay if I'm not keeping up. One pump at a time, this too shall pass. Small victories ahead.

♦♦♦♦♦

FEBRUARY 25

I've been forcing myself to use my pumping time for deep breathing and prayer. It's becoming the best twenty minutes of my day, and it doesn't hurt bringing those cookies for extra emotional support.

Pumptime meditations. This could be a whole business. Is it weird I'm now taking a picture of Isa into the pumping room with me? I've heard staring at your child's picture helps with production.

The whole thing feels shady, but the meditation part helps.

Yeah, I need to reframe this experience.

The first time I stripped down at work I felt like a whore. I was like, "This is SO WRONG." Now I shed like a pony in the spring.

Prayers and ponies. Whatever it takes to feed the village.

♦♦♦♦♦

MARCH 6

So, I'm taking home all pump parts and cleaning them every day. This can't be right. It takes hours.

You only have to clean the parts that come in contact with the milk.

So not the three-foot long tubes?

Nope. Those can stay on the machine.

What about the backflow protectors?

Nope. Those stay too.

That is life changing.

Always here to help.

♦♦♦♦♦

MARCH 12

How's the "Don't Kill Your Husband" book?

It's sitting on my shelf with all the other things I don't have time to read. I can't even keep my eyes open at the end of the night.

Have you seen "Working Moms" on Netflix?

Oh yes. And "The Letdown."

I think "The Letdown" is Australian so it doesn't have that American happiness to it. It's just the raw dirt. You either die laughing or hysterically cry.

I know. I cried.

I had to turn it off when the nanny secretly gave the child formula, claiming the mom's breast milk was nonfat skim.

Have you started formula yet?

Still on the shelf. It's growing moths by now.

The misery. I have to let go of the whole milk supply thing.

Let me know how you figure that one out.

◆ ◆ ◆ ◆ ◆

I was a formula-fed child. It was all the rage in the '80s. My mother never breastfed me, convinced she was giving me the top nutrients in town with the new-fangled Nestle. Now, the pendulum has swung back to the way of Mama Nature, complete with marketing ads of "Breast is Best" and guidelines to suckle your infant indefinitely.

I was determined to do this. After all, how hard could it be? Our ancestors fed whole tribes of babies for centuries; certainly, I could feed one child. My great-great-grandmother had seven or eight children by the time she turned forty! How weak am I if I can't feed one?

Now, I have lots of friends who could never breastfeed. Others who said it wasn't for them. I hold ZERO judgment toward them—why can't I offer myself the same grace?

As moms, we all hang our hats on different totems that make us feel like "good moms." For some, it's mastering the homemade birthday cake. For others, it's hosting neighborhood soccer matches in their yard. Some moms are top organic chefs, others need to sew their own clothes, others quit their careers for their children—everyone has their THING or actually LIST OF THINGS to feel like a GOOD mom.

But when we say GOOD, we really mean PERFECT. We believe to our core that love abounds when we master our lists. On the flip side, if we don't, we have wrecked our child's lives. We not only had a mom fail, we ARE mom failures.

What a giant load of diaper filth! Perfection isn't sustainable. In fact, it's not even attainable. No one can do it all. No one ever has or ever could. But wanting to show the utmost love, our inner perfectionists have a hard time believing this.

Surely, we can be the exception, right?

Actually, there are no exceptions. Trust me, I've checked. I've spent decades of my life resenting this fact, but God doesn't seem to budge on it. There is NO perfect life, wife, mom, dad, partner, baby, husband, house, or handbag. Perfection is an illusion, an alluring mirage like fat-free ice cream that looks too good to be true. And trust me, it is! That mirage is filled with nasty fake lies that will kill you and make you fatter (because you will stress eat trying to keep up with perfection).

But if we can't be perfect, what's our next best option? Particularly when other moms still seem to hold up this mirage so well... particularly THAT mom who shows up with organic homemade made-from-scratch muffins to EVERY outing. I mean, who the hell has time for that? And why isn't God passing her the "nobody is perfect" memo?

The psychoanalyst and pediatrician D.W. Winnicott wrote extensively on the illusion of perfection in motherhood. He found (surprise, surprise) there are no perfect moms, but there are plenty of GOOD ENOUGH mothers. Winnicott studied thousands of new families, watching mom after mom topple in complete surrender to her baby's needs. He then watched many of those moms awaken and realize that such a system isn't sustainable. At this point, the mom gets stuck in a quandary: attend to her child's every request or lower her standards.

No woman wants to lower her standards. We are taught from childhood to raise our benchmarks, not lower them. We reach for the stars and aim for the heavens, and nothing will stop us from raising the bar. But sometimes the bar we set is not humanly possible for any known human, let alone ourselves. I don't care if Sally Sweetbread appears to do it all. She can't. It's another lie. She is in this dilemma too, wrestling against her standards.

But this wrestle is the start of freedom, because this dilemma is the birth of the Good Enough Mother. Just as babies grow, mothers mature too and, eventually, we learn that perfection is not an option. Nor do we even want it to be.

While it may not appear so from the onset, the Good Enough Mother (GEM) is healthier than the Gotta-Be-Perfect (GBP) mom. The GEM has ideals but knows not all of them can be reached. She aims for the stars knowing she is only five foot two. She trusts the high motivations of her heart but doesn't beat herself up when she can't accomplish them. She lets her best attempt be good enough. She's honest, messy, and REAL.

Meanwhile, Mrs. GBP is not perfect, but can't admit it either, so it's double-trouble all around. Her main goal is to appear flawless and never ever fail. From the outside, her mothering is pristine, but she's drowning in smoke and mirrors and needs a little grace. We all do.

Children actually need to experience failure. They need their caregivers to fail them in small, forgivable ways so they learn the world is imperfect.

People are imperfect. They can be imperfect. And despite it all, the love goes on. Failure lets our children know that THEY are good enough, that they don't need to perfect to be loved. This is how people become resilient humans. We fall, we learn we are okay, we see are still lovable, and we get up and try again. We take risks, embrace imperfections, and love through thick and thin.

It feels scary to switch hats from the GBP to the GEM, but there's freedom on the other side. Mrs. GBP is a façade that is bound to crack. You can only pretend to be perfect for so long until someone or something pulls the curtain on you, and then the show is done. Meanwhile, the Good Enough Mom is flesh and blood. She may be tattered, but she's proud of her scars. She's the real Velveteen rabbit, with taggled hair and eyes that fall out occasionally, but she's legit, she's true, and true love is the story that gets remembered.

It's time to be the story that gets remembered.

♦♦♦♦♦

MARCH 18

It's official. I'm starting formula. Thank you for hearing all my rants.
I'm a true inspiration. #momfail
You are a true guilt absolver.
Why the sudden switch?
I read about the Good Enough Mother. And maybe it's my working mom hormones kicking in, but I suddenly saw Isa as a sweet, hungry child, staring at me like, "Mom, when are you gonna get over yourself and give me the Holle!"
You feel okay?
Yes, mostly because she's six months. That was the amended EBF goal. I'll still nurse her; I'll just supplement rather than spend all day pumping two ounces.
Do you think we will always set these unattainable mom goals?
You mean they don't end with the breastfeeding saga?
Maybe that is the hard lesson we are supposed to learn. Maybe goals are meant to be broken.
Or aim high but swing low.
I'm bad at that.
We all are.

♦♦♦♦♦

MARCH 19

So, I announced to Jeff that I'm okay with formula.

What did he say? Was he so proud of you?

He said he'd been waiting for me to get over the "ego of milk."

Um, did you smack him?

I cried. That was worse.

Well, my dear husband told me today that I might want to clean the bathroom floor more regularly . . . as it was covered with his hair.

I hope you swept it into a heart shape, so he can see your true love for him.

Gag me.

I swear, Jeff has not skipped one daily shower since Isa was born. I'm lucky if I shave my legs quarterly.

Well, I can braid the hair on my legs now it's so long. Oh, and Mateo sleeps through the night EVERY night and still complains about being tired.

I could slug him in his perfect sleep for you?

It's like training a husband and baby at the same time.

To counter, I'm trying a new marital strategy called, "Do less and let the husband fill in the gaps."

How's that working?

It's frustrating the hell out of me because he doesn't do the gaps right. Take the diaper bag, for instance. I always pack it. But when I ask him to pack it, he follows me around asking what goes inside it twenty times, and I just want to scream, "Learn your daughter! She needs diapers and wipes and a change of clothes." And then somehow three hundred jackets get shoved in the diaper bag (in case she gets cold) and guess who has to unpack said diaper bag and refold her entire wardrobe?

Remember when we talked about the unseen cognitive load of moms? Maybe you are still doing too much then.

It's not a huge cognitive load to learn the diaper bag list. And I don't have time to mansplain it.

I've started doing absolutely ZERO around the house unless I directly need it. And thus, indirectly, leaving it for Mateo to do.

Brilliant. Does anything get done?

Not yet, but I've also started phrasing things like, "Will you do x, y, z WHILE I NURSE Enora, so he realizes that I'm doing something for our child and maybe he can pitch in in other ways.

When he pitches in, does he do it right?

Well, my new mantra is, "It's not how I would do it, but at least the baby's still alive." That calms the inner madness a quarter of the time.

Ah, yes. The Good Enough Husband. I'm working on that vision too.
Me too. I've been so hard on Mateo. I really do adore him.
I know you do. I adore Jeff too. I just don't always understand him.
Have we turned into Momzillas?
Is that a step up or step down from Bridezillas?
I skipped the Bridezilla stage as we eloped. So maybe I get double the Momzilla time.

◆◆◆◆◆

MARCH 24

We started solids today. Avocados and bananas here we come.
Real food for the win!
Although I was looking online at portion sizing, and I'm confused.
Never look online. Says the woman who always looks online.
Nobody knows.
Everyone just pretends to know.
Do you think that's a mom epidemic too? Moms just keep pretending to know crap and pretending so hard it makes other moms feel bad for NOT knowing. When really, nobody knows?
Sometimes, I even feel like dropping the baby.
Me too.
Don't ever confess that one out loud.
Nope. It goes to the grave.
I wouldn't actually drop her, of course.
No need to clarify. I get it.
And that's the beauty of girlfriends.

◆◆◆◆◆

Here's what I do know. Motherhood requires math, and it requires math in a life moment of brain fog. And it's not the romantic fog of Irish hillsides. It's the clogged exhaust of rusty Fords. I can't remember where I left my sunglasses most days, let alone complex arithmetic formulas. So, when motherhood hands me math, I tape a list to my fridge that looks like this:
Solids: start at 4–6 months
Baby sleep: 17–19 hours a day
Mom sleep: 0

Breast milk keeps at room temp: 4–6 hours
Breast milk keeps in fridge: 3 days
Breast milk keeps in freezer: 3–6 months
Breast milk keeps in deep freezer: 6–12 months
Formula ration: 1 tablespoon to 1 ounce of water, stir at 101 degrees
First solid portion: 2–4 tablespoons
Daily milk: 36 ounces max in a 24-hour period
Daily wine: 8 ounces every day Mom survives
Daily time to myself: Carve out 15 minutes. I promise you can find it.

♦ ♦ ♦ ♦ ♦

MARCH 31

Rice cereal is the BEST invention. I should have thought of this months ago. She loves it! I'll send you a picture.

Look at it all over her chin! Wait, are you feeding her with a mini gelato spoon?

It's the smallest spoon we have. I haven't made it to the store yet to buy a real baby spoon.

It's her size. I bet there's a market for that.

She slept a little longer stretch after eating it yesterday. Fuller belly = sleepy belly.

We tried the water trick last night and Enora slept longer too.

What's the water trick?

When she wakes, we gave her water in a bottle rather than milk. It's an attempt to night wean. She didn't even notice the difference.

That's amazing.

Mateo did it. He gave her one ounce, and she conked out. I'm not really sure what happened. No one is. Whatever Mateo does in the night is a mystery to everyone including him, because he also doesn't remember.

I don't remember my days very well, but I remember every second of every night, as girlfriend still gets up all night long.

Same here. I bet our girls are texting each other in the middle of the night.

I hope their texts are more coherent than ours.

Hey, Isa. How's your rice cereal? Dance party at dawn? Love, Enora.

♦ ♦ ♦ ♦ ♦

APRIL 1

So, I talked to my pediatrician. She had A LOT of opinions on solids. She said to give the babes small meals FIVE times a day. Steel-cut oats are the least processed so start there. Boil, add pureed veg or fruit, then blend.

Holy shite, that's a lot of work. And you are gonna do that every day?

Who knows? She also said to start peanut butter and eggs now to avoid allergies. Next month, start lean proteins. At eight months, start legumes because the cells in their bowels change around then, and they can digest them better. Berries come after the first birthday, as well as dairy and honey.

I need to get out my whiteboard again.

Don't you dare!

So seriously, are you doing all that?

I'll start with the best intentions.

I forget my own lunch at school. There's no way I can pack five mini-meals for her a day.

Makes breastfeeding seem so easy.

✦✦✦✦✦

APRIL 2

So, I just talked to my uber-organic sister, and she said hold off on ALL grains. Babies can't properly digest them, and they sit in the gut and wreak havoc on their tummies. It can actually give them grain allergies.

Really?

She sent me this link: why-babies-shouldn't-eat-grains-and-what-to-feed-them-instead

But she's sleeping an extra few hours on the cereal!

I know. We are all back in the gutter. My husband just sent me another article: why-babies-can't-digest-starch. I'm getting bombarded on all sides.

OMG. How hard is it to feed or not-feed a little human?

Evidently, it's quite controversial. She also said to avoid rice due to the arsenic, even in the organic stuff. If you can't avoid it, add stewed prunes to prevent constipation.

Did your doctor say how often to try new foods?

Every three days. So, you introduce avocados for three days in a row, then bananas for three, etc. We just finished three days of peas.

Are you pureeing all this stuff?

Yes. I'm stewing the veggies and fruits in a pot, mashing those babies, then fridging them in mason jars. I also got some refillable pouches, but really this is all an experiment.

Wow. I'll churn this up for her, but I'm having frozen pizza for dinner. Glad I added Costco to my Good Enough Mother list.

I'm still working on that addition.

♦♦♦♦♦

APRIL 5

My body has turned into a B-grade sci-fi show. I'm that mom zombie who always has plugged ducts.

I remember that character! She's badass.

In today's episode, one finally unplugged.

Hopefully that's the final episode.

I'm sure my body will call for an encore.

If they even made a film about postpartum pleasantries, no one would watch it.

I mean, I can't watch horror.

Mombies! Their eyelids are painted open one eyelash at a time, but they haven't slept in years!

Your sleepless mombie could fight my plugged duct mombie.

I'd fall asleep mid-swing.

You are right. No one would watch this film.

In fact, can you remove me from a starring role?

In eighteen years, but by then we will be weeping mombies, wondering where all the time went.

The cruel circle of life.

♦♦♦♦♦

APRIL 6

So my chiropractor, who is normally a godsend, went on and on today about the dangers of the Bimbo and the Ergo.

Well, bimbos are quite dangerous . . .

The Bumbo, I mean. That little training seat kids sit in. My mother-in-law gave it to me to help Isa develop her core.

I need an adult Bumbo to develop my core.

I'll give your ours, because I now have to get rid of them. According to her, they force babies' hips into unnatural positions.

Aren't babies uber flexible?

That's what I said! She basically said, if I use them, Isa could walk funny. I can't win!

I'm realizing every stage has its own formal guilt trip. To eat grain or not eat grain. To Ergo or not to Ergo.

These are her favorite contraptions. They give me moments of peace!

Remember in college when we learned of Maslow's hierarchy of needs in Psych 101?

When we would sit in the back and stalk the hotty RA?

Yes, that sweet Joseph boy. Beyond him, do you remember that cute little needs pyramid? You need food, shelter, sleep to exist—that's the bottom of the triangle.

Failing at those.

Exactly. Only once those are covered can you proceed to the middle triangle tier.

Remind me what those are?

Love and self-esteem. Then at the very top of that triangle are thriving ideals.

Well, wouldn't we all like to be there!

But I'm not in thriving mode.

I'm scratching survival every day.

Exactly. See, we aren't in an IDEAL world, Mr. Maslow. We are surviving, and my Ergo gives me twenty minutes of sanity so I'm not giving it up.

Sane moms make sane babies.

Will I forgive myself if she walks with a limp one day?

She won't.

And bimbos give me ten minutes of freedom!

Bimbos do tend to do that.

Bumbos. Darn this Greek baby talk.

I hear you. I've concluded that I will stop judging other moms while simultaneously stop listening to other moms.

Can we hold each other to that? Parenting is already an uphill battle without banning the Bumbo.

Let's start trusting our guts and set the bar low. Like Dead-Sea-level low. As long as our daughters don't become bimbos, I'd say we succeeded.

◆◆◆◆◆

Speaking of ideals, plan on tossing your shoe collection once a baby joins your world. During pregnancy, you'll stare at your heels in disdain and start drooling over cushioned orthopedics. Postpartum, the cute shoe desire returns, but now your feet are obese. To all those years of shoe bargains say, "Adios." No more size seven. Hello, plus-size Keds.

If that wasn't enough, your arches collapse from the extra watermelon you carried around, so you gotta find support from the ground up. Instead of fashion, you start researching Temper-Pedic shoe inserts. Au revoir, high heels. Ain't no baby being carted in stilettos. Hello, foam Converse.

There is one option to skirt the shoe genocide. I call it imaginary play. You simply PRETEND your pre-baby shoes still fit and shove those suckers into those Vince Camutos. Warning: There is a price for this fantasy, which is why podiatry exists, and I'm now frequenting my local doc. I bring the average client age down by four decades, but at least those shoes still fit. #neversaydie

◆◆◆◆◆

APRIL 10

Do you have any libido left? And why are husbands so annoying? These are my questions.

I'm not the right person to ask.

You are my ONLY person to ask.

Let's just say I'm on my way to the therapist again right now. I mean, parenting a little human with the opposite sex is entirely illogical. The way men and women view the world are night and day different.

It would be so much easier to raise babies in pods of women. Jeff and I had another fight over the diaper bag.

Oh wait, did he ask you what it needs?

For the 400th time.

It's not rocket science.

I told him I was going to laminate a packing list and tape it to his hand.

It's maddening. It's like the male brain literally can only focus on one task at a time.

And then they get mad at us for multitasking.

If we didn't multitask, our family would starve and trip over piles of teething beads.

I know. I can track every place my husband and her go because there's a line of dirty diapers and toys in their wake . . . which will stay there until I pick them up.

Meanwhile, we cook, clean, and bounce babies on our knees, while typing with our right hand.

And organizing the world with our left. I don't need much. I'm just trying to teach him the art of the grasp. For example, when I leave a room, I look around and GRASP misplaced toys to return to where I'm going. I pick up a dirty diaper as I'm passing the trash. I grab the old bottle as I'm headed to the kitchen. I'm not asking him to make extra trips. Just maximize the journey he's already on.

Good luck with that. If I can't teach my husband the grasp for his own towels, I doubt I can teach him to grasp our child's stuff.

It's not hard. When you bathe the baby, look around. Maybe even drain the water out of the tub so I don't find it the next morning with a fresh layer of Burt's Bee soap scum.

To dream of drains. My therapist keeps telling me to stop trying to understand each other.

What's the alternative?

Respect that you each have your own way of doing things with the baby.

But what if their way is plain wrong?

That's where my head goes. But she says he may never do it my way, and that's okay.

So, we have to respect them doing it the wrong way?

Apparently. And pretend the wrong way is a creative, alternative path.

Are we arrogant?

It would only be arrogant if we weren't doing it the right way.

Let's ask our daughters in twenty years. If they need therapy, we can just bill their fathers.

✦✦✦✦✦

APRIL 16

Speaking of therapy, I should probably go again.

Honestly, it's the best decision I've made postpartum. If I could pass on any advice to a new mom, I'd say book ten sessions before you even give birth.

I'm on it. I also have spring break coming up for work, and Jeff has a work conference in Mexico.

Are you going?

Yes, our first international parenting trip.

Viva la Resistencia! That will refresh you! See, small pieces of life are returning!

Therapy and Mexico sound like a regular Margaritaville.

Pass the salt, please.

♦ ♦ ♦ ♦ ♦

APRIL 24

So, I made a four-page packing list for traveling with a child.

Holy smokes. And you say I'm the planner.

It's actually because I'm a loser. I lose objects so I need to write everything down or else it evaporates.

I'll send you a travel article I just read: "Six Ways to Recover from Your Child's Mid-Air Meltdown." Helpful tips for flying.

How about mid-Tuesday meltdowns?

Midnight meltdowns?

Midlife new-mom crisis?

I need all the lists I can get. We fly tomorrow.

♦ ♦ ♦ ♦ ♦

Let's chat vacation. I'd heard the word "vacation" goes out the window for a while after children, like twenty years a while. You still take excursions, but they get rebranded as "trips." You now trip to the Grand Canyon or Canada. You trip to the beach.

But you never vacate anything.

My husband and I are seasoned travelers and late parents, so we assure ourselves this rule won't apply to us. We will relish the Mexican landscape. Our child will be bilingual by the time we return. She will be the sole baby that never wails on a plane.

Oh wait, have you met my daughter?

Magically, she becomes the Good Enough Baby and never makes a peep on the plane. It's a true miracle from heaven. Post-flight, we quickly relax into vacation mode. Jeff's work conference is at a beautiful beachside resort. The water is sparkling blue. The temperature is warm but not too hot.

We are VACATING life.

I grab my beach towel, spread it gently on the sand, and glance around with Isa in arms. Beside me are dozens of couples, sipping drinks and spooning on the sand. No one dares make eye contact—they wave at Isa but not me. Within minutes, one couple moves their chairs away from our blanket. Another couple leaves altogether. It takes a second to register, but then their cues hit me.

I've become that woman no one wants on their vacation. People flee the country to get away from their kids. No one wants to sip cocktails near a baby, no matter how scrumptious her cheeks are.

I pull my baby close and tell her they don't understand her glory. I remind her my thighs have rolls too, but hers are way cuter. I tell her she is the princess of the beach.

I look around at one couple still nearby. They smile and ask, "How old is your child?"

"She's seven months," I say.

"We have a seven-month-old too, but we left her at home with grandma." And then they kiss and prance off to the ocean. The husband pulls his wife obscenely close, as though they are newly dating, and I try not to notice her postpartum six-pack.

Smile politely, Jen. Just pull up your revamped maternity dress, now tied up with a super sexy scrunchy, and be glad at least your boobs are still swollen. You are on a trip. Look on the bright side.

You are also at a resort that is hosting a bikini boot camp. Note to self: Don't bring yourself to a bikini boot camp when you can't sport a bikini. Further note: Don't bring your husband to his own work conference based at a bikini boot camp.

Okay, I may not have a six-pack anymore, or ever, but there's no need to cry a river. There is still lots of fun to be had. I pull out the hotel brochure and look at the list of suggested activities—scuba, yoga, surf camp, volleyball, tennis, visiting ruins, swimming in the cenotes.

I want to do ALL of them.

Isa coos and looks deep into my eyes. She grabs the brochure and starts to eat it. You are right, Child. I can do none of those activities now. And some days, I don't need to do any of them. And other days, like right now, I want to do each one. This is a short season, I remind myself. One day, we can adventure, but for today, we can TRIP together on this beautiful beach.

I need to text Sam.

◆◆◆◆◆

APRIL 26

Are you there? This is the most romantic place I've seen in years, and I suddenly want romance again with my husband. Except, we have no babysitter.

The libido always hits at the worst times.

I also have this sudden urge to workout, but I can't participate in any of the activities with the little one. I checked into childcare options, but those don't start until age three. Is it wrong to want to exercise?

It's probably the healthiest thing you can do.

Look, everyone was right. Vacations with babies are not vacations. They are lovely, but is it too much to ask for a free day with a girlfriend? Can we plan a getaway? I'm headed to the East Coast this summer to visit my mom. That's not far from you in Boston.

Maybe we could meet in NYC? We could bring the girls! They could meet each other, and we can baby them around the subway like hip cool city moms?

(Extended pause)

Why don't we try for a childless meetup?

That sounds epic.

♦♦♦♦♦

APRIL 28

I found a semi-nice hotel room in NY.

Anything with four walls sounds luxurious. Remember, I'm in paradise right now and the only thing keeping me going is this idea.

Fresh sheets!

Uninterrupted sleep!

Wait, who is watching the babes?

I'll ask my mom to watch her for the night. Could your mom do the same?

Yes.

Are we ready to be away from our babies? They will be ten months by then.

(Extended pause)

Hell, yeah.

♦♦♦♦♦

Mexico taught me a great lesson: my child hates my boobs. She has from the get-go, but the Riviera made it real. I'm surrounded by beautiful Mexican mamas, holding their placid children at their breasts. It's like a Frida Kahlo painting—pure, innocent, fertile, and docile. I offer my child milk and she spurns me, and meanwhile in the meadow, all of Mexico breastfeeds in a sweet Latin lullaby.

In those quiet, twilight hours where Isa has nursed in peace, I stroke her head and find rest. It's tender. It's calm. It's bonding. But my child's also asleep. I'm bonding with someone in dreamland.

It took months to supplement with formula. And now I face the next Good Enough Mom question: to wean or not to wean. When I was pregnant, I attended breastfeeding circles where women held their preteen children, still attached to the boob. These kids clutched their nipple in one hand and the "New York Times" in the other, which they could read, thanks to the power of breast milk.

I want Isa to read the "Times," but weaning is a one-way street. You hand in the keys, dry up, and exchange your nursing bras for a padded collection. So long, girls. Hello, sag.

In my own mom tribe, breast is not only best, it's Bible. It's as though Moses walked down from the holy mountain with two tablets and one breast. For the men, he read the ten tableted commandments, because let's face it— women already knew not to steal or start wars. But for women, he held up the giant boob, and said, "Let there be milk." And there was milk. And it was good.

In modern religion, there are entire businesses dedicated to breast milk remembrance. I came across one online company that preserves your milk into a jewel. You send in an ounce of your liquid, and they craft it into a pearl. Their tagline: to remember the bond that was closer than any other.

In all honesty, there is nothing about me that wants to commemorate this process, which is why it's time to wean.

True, breast milk is medicinal. It's that rare delicacy the pharmaceutical companies haven't been able to reproduce with integrity. They can't grow it or GMO it. There are no breast milk kegs or vats. Why? Because children are supposed to LOVE boobs. They are supposed to go wild for them, like teenage boys with jaws dropped to the floor begging, "Gimme, gimme, gimme."

My sweet girl has never fed in peace except on the bottle. She screams, wails, and arches her back on me. It's time to lay this season to rest and give her the peace she's been asking for. Alright imported German formula, I'm diving all-in for you. Thank you, Mexico, for paving the way.

♦♦♦♦♦

MAY 1

Mother's Day is coming up. What do you want?

A solo trip to the bathroom, an unlimited Amazon spree, a leather tote that can double as a diaper bag, and sleep.

OMG. We have the same list. I'll tell your husband if you tell mine.

Done. Are you back yet?

Yes, parenting again on the pavement rather than the sand.

I told you. Traveling with a kid is doing the same drill, just with a large airfare bill in your pocket.

♦ ♦ ♦ ♦ ♦

MAY 2

I resolved to wean in Mexico. Baby girl and I are both ready.

Wow. That's a huge step. I wish I was there.

She's happy with her bottle, and it's time to stop disrupting that.

That's honorable.

But then today, she looks up at me while nursing and says, "Mama!" Now I can't quit.

Yes, you can. Have you read that Jimmy Fallon book, "Everything is Mama."

Every damn day. At the end of it, you know what she always says?

"Dada!"

Yes, except today. She's onto me.

Our kids will always have our number. Trust your decision.

What a concept.

Do you know about cabbage leaves? If you place them on your boobs, it dries up milk production.

I knew cabbage was good for something.

Cabbage is good for many things. Ask any Korean.

♦ ♦ ♦ ♦ ♦

MAY 6

First day in weeks without a plug on either side!

Mother's Day came early this year!

And Enora slept all night long ALL week.

Victory is yours. Maybe we don't need real Mother's Day gifts?
(extended pause)
I'll text your hubs. You text mine.

◆◆◆◆◆

MAY 24

P.S. I weaned.
PROUD OF YOU.
It was a non-event. She barely noticed. I handed her a bottle instead, and she didn't bat an eyelash.
Wow. All that torture for THAT?
I know. Months of unrelenting torment!
How are your boobs?
Fine. I never produced enough milk to clog anything.
I hate you. Wait, aren't you done with teaching soon?
Just a few more weeks until summer break.
Double celebration!
Onward and upward.

◆◆◆◆◆

MAY 28

I met up with my mom group, and I'm the only weaner.
No regrets, remember?
They all looked like a Madonna and child painting, gently suckling baby Jesus and bringing peace to all humankind.
And what did you look like when you breastfed?
A tattered figure in a Dali scene.
You did the right thing.
Maybe I could have tried harder.
Stop it.
I've read you can jumpstart your boobs again by eating fennel stalks and steaming in a hot shower.
I'm cutting you off. You are done. Go look at Renaissance paintings if you need the romantic vision. Or I'll send you a picture of my nipple needle operation this morning.

I can't believe you are still pricking yourself.

Almost daily.

This is how people get pregnant again, isn't it? I'm less than a day out, and I've forgotten all the horror.

Exactly. Women are great at repressing the details.

♦♦♦♦♦

When you say goodbye to a phase in motherhood, what is gone becomes iconic. It's like that classmate you never really liked, but as graduation rolls around, he becomes that chum you sway with, shed a tear over, and scratch his phone number in your yearbook.

Stay cool, breastfeeding. I'll miss you. Everything looks rosy in the rear-view mirror. Soon, the first year of my daughter's life will be over. Cabbage leaves or not, I'll fold up her onesies one by one and remember none of this madness, only crazy mad love.

♦♦♦♦♦

JUNE 1

I'm two weeks late.

No . . .

I'm blaming it on the weaning.

But you only weaned a week ago.

I need a pregnancy test.

♦♦♦♦♦

JUNE 2

I took two pregnancy tests. Both negative.

Phew.

Can you imagine?

I think I may just crawl into a cave and never leave.

How Plato of you. Jeff and his sister are fifteen months apart. That means we would be six months pregnant already.

Um, I put in an IUD the day I got "released" to have sex again. And then I told my husband I wasn't cleared for another six weeks after that.

You clear yourself honey when you want to.
What are you doing for that whole rigmarole?
I'm on birth control now.
Good.
Plus condoms.
Even better.
Plus abstinence.
The triple whammy.
I still don't know why I'm late.
I think our cycles will be confused for a while.
I know a few other things that will be confused for a while.

♦♦♦♦♦

JUNE 14

Hotel is officially booked! We have twenty-four hours of baby-free living ahead in NYC. I chose a hotel with a no-refunds policy too, so there's no turning back.

That is magic. And now that I'm a free woman, I won't even have to pump!

We have a true VACATION ahead.

What I really need is a few weeks to download with you, but I'll take the day.

We take what we can.

It's the little things.

♦♦♦♦♦

JUNE 15

I feel off.
What's ON even feel like?
Who knows, but I feel like I'm PMSing without the chocolate cravings. I'm weepy.
Are you okay?
I'm not sure. I feel like I wrecked it.
What's "it?"
The marriage. The body. The good life.

What's going on?

I think Mexico threw me through a loop. It was the same work confer-ence we went to last year, glowing and pregnant, sipping mocktails poolside while eagerly reading books about parenting. Everyone rubbed my stomach and opened doors for me. This year, we were the haggard couple with the loud baby. No one opened doors for us. My bright eyes are bloodshot. I framed last year's vacation photos. I deleted this year's pics.

The comparison of pre-baby and post-baby life is the worst. I just started a book by the Gottmans called "Baby Makes Three."

Is it hopeful?

It says sixty-seven percent of marriages go off the rails with kids.

Encouraging.

My therapist recommended it. She says the marriage often falls back-burner to the baby, and while the marriage can be a great source of strength, it often becomes an extra place of angst.

My husband gets energy from the baby-makes-three pod. I love fam-ily time, but I'm also wired to need solo time or even a date night. Neither's happening.

Not even in Mexico?

It was beautiful, but he had to work the whole time. I saw him for lunch and dinner. Why host a work conference on a beach if there is no time to pause work and enjoy it?

Who knows.

My sole hope is girl time with you. I need a happiness refresher.

I've heard that a man's happiness skyrockets after a new baby and a woman's plummets for quite a while. Eventually, the mom's happiness in-creases to more than it was originally.

When does that happen?

I think at the grandparent stage—so if our daughters are like us, forty years from now.

A long-term investment portfolio.

At least stocks grow.

♦♦♦♦♦

JUNE 18

Okay, so I've been teary EVERY DAY since I weaned.

Do you think weaning messed with your hormones?

Yes. I Googled it. I think I have PWD. Post-weaning depression.

Is that a thing? I'm never weaning now.

It's a rather common thing but hasn't gotten the press of postpartum depression.

What are the symptoms?

The same as PPD—tears, night sweats, lack of energy, irritability, anxiety, and insomnia (most of which I've had since the birth). But for some women, the weaning hormones can bring on the worst of it. I've never felt this fragile. I mean, I've been tired since day one, but not weepy. I've redone my mascara twice already today.

At least you are wearing mascara.

And to top it off, I keep getting Instagram ads for the belly band I wear— that corset thing that is supposed to pull my stomach back together.

Is the band helping?

Slowly, but look at their advertising. I'll send you the link. It's postpartum Barbie.

There's no way that woman is even old enough to birth a child!

Or ever even had one.

She deserves to die.

I'm eating a bon-bon in her memory right now.

So much is genetics. That's what I keep telling myself.

I hate genetics. My hormones and motherhood don't mix well.

Can you call your doctor?

She's gonna think I'm crazy.

That's the irony of women's health. It's still steeped in medieval remnants of the hysterical woman. You are not CRAZY. The system is set up to make you feel crazy. Your body is being hijacked right now by your biochemistry.

Can I ask the hijackers to land me on an exotic safari?

Only if you take me with you.

♦♦♦♦♦

JUNE 20

Okay, the weepy has ended. Now, I'm just annoyed ALL the time. At dawn. At dusk. With Jeff. With life. I need a kickboxing class.

Sign me up. Can you get to one?

Likely not. Who has time?

What's free time?

Does your husband take breaks from parenting?

Yes, which makes me madder.

I get it. Jeff was watching ten minutes of TV while I was scrubbing bottles after work last night, and he asked me to come sit with him . . . But then, my love, how will the bottles get washed? Or the baby eat? He says I need to BE and not DO.

I'd love to just BE. But then we would live in a pigsty, and no one would eat.

I just want to punch something. Is that too much to ask?

Hey, my exercise has been reduced to stroller pushing.

Speaking of strollers, I suddenly hate mine, along with everything else in my life. I bought it for the one-handed "fold," but I should have stuck with my gut and got the travel-sized Yoyo.

Always follow your gut. Look, when we get to NYC, we can go on runs and punch pillows and shower all day long.

What do we do until then?

Lots of texting.

◆◆◆◆◆

JUNE 22

So, I was inspired by our self-care chat. I put her to bed early and attempted a workout. And right there, with the weights in my hands, I start bawling again. I was sobbing on my patio over five-pound dumbbells for NO REASON. I'm checking myself into the looney bin.

Oh honey, let the tears out.

What is wrong with me?

It's the hormones.

But maybe the hormones tell the truth. I should be loving this whole mom gig, but I'm not. And all I feel toward my beautiful husband is straight murder.

Does Jeff feel the same way?

Not at all. He only gets upset if I have forty-nine requests of him, and I point out the one he missed.

Mateo is the same. He's only mad when I'm mad at him. And it's been an exceptionally maddening week.

This is a season, right?

Every mom I know tells me they look back at the diaper days with fondness.

Do you think you will?

Ask me in a few years.

◆◆◆◆◆

JULY 1

I'm losing it. Isa needs to start sleeping, I need to start sleeping, or one of us has to go.
What's the plan?
I called my doctor. If that doesn't work, I'm erecting a tent in the yard.
For you or the baby?
I'll arm wrestle her for it. Moral of the story? Don't ever wean. It bites you either way.
#100yearsoldstillmakingmilk

◆◆◆◆◆

No one ever plans on motherhood involving pharmaceutical interventions. You don't become a mom to feel rickety. Motherhood is supposed to be full of pastel blankets and bathtime bliss, not brink-of-death insanity. But I can no longer crawl in bed afraid of the night, nor can I cry all day from exhaustion. I have to mother, and I have to work.

I have to move beyond this.

I remember the moment I brought my baby home from the hospital. She was swaddled in a perfect pink paisley wrap and smelled as divine as creme brûlée. It was the full harvest moon. My husband and I put on a lullaby playlist and stood outside, amazed at the miracle of love resting in our arms. I breastfed her sweetly, amazed at her ability to latch, convinced she was the next Da Vinci. We swaddled her gently in her bassinet and hugged each other into bed, ready to rest.

She slept soundly for three hours. I fed her again, suckling her to my breast and laying her back down to rest. I was too excited to sleep. All throughout the night, I stared at her glory, unable to stop pondering her. By morning, I still hadn't fallen asleep.

This was excitement; I was sure of it.

When you have a baby, everyone tells you how in love you will be, and their predictions are right. I was enamored with every toe, facial expression, and coo. Sure, I was warned of the sleepless nights, but there was so much love to fuel it.

What they don't tell you is how, even if your baby sleeps, you might not sleep . . . ever again.

I was convinced the sleeplessness was just sheer elation. I was a mom! I had an amazing daughter. So, I put on my headphones before bed and listened to a meditation. I prayed every night for rest. I bought medical-grade sleep masks, Googled healthy sleep habits, and turned off all tech past dinner. I cut out sugar (which was worse than slow-drip water torture). I practiced yoga savasana, slowly contracting the muscles in my body to unwind. I lit candles and waved sage throughout the house. I carved out a rigid sleep window, stumbling to bed at the same time every night, but nothing ever worked.

"Rest your mind," my husband says, as though I've skipped that step.

"Sleep when the baby sleeps," the doctor says, as though I enjoy staying up.

"Have proper bedtime habits," others say. Yes, thank you. I now wear blue-blocking glasses past sunset. I take magnesium with dinner, melatonin with dessert, and chamomile as my nightcap. My aromatherapy diffuser is overflowing with stress relief oil, a bedtime blend of lavender and frankincense.

"Have you tried reading?" my mom asks. And so, I read . . . an entire book.

"What about doing dishes or some other mindless activity?" others suggest. Sure, I'll try that, and then by dawn, I'm up cleaning counters.

"Try boring podcasts!" And by episode six, I just don't have strength for more of "The Daily."

It's been almost a year of this strange twilight, where I crawl in bed at dusk and fall asleep at dawn. After a year of two hours each night, the world starts to fuzz. Top that with new weaning hormones, and I'm one giant blubberfest.

Dear loved ones, thank you for your advice. I'll try all of your tips, but can I give you a piece of advice? Please don't give me any more advice. Please just say, "I'm sorry, that sounds miserable; we will find a solution."

This is postpartum. When you mention you are hurting, others stare at you with empathy, but what they really mean is, "What's wrong with you? What's wrong with your mind? I didn't go through this in my postpartum period, so something must be wrong with YOU." It's a weird case of blaming the mom, once again.

I'd give ANYTHING for this to go away, to have my health back, to consolidate the memories I'm making with my daughter. I then tried Benadryl, Advil-PM, CBD oil, night-time vitamin tinctures, acupuncture, and self-acupressure points. The list of remedies next to my bed took up my whole nightstand.

And still, nothing.

Humbled, I head to the doctors. After a long intake and a referral to stay in therapy, she puts me on progesterone, a hormone that plummets during the postpartum period, and hands me a prescription for anti-anxiety assistance. Within days, I remember how to fall asleep again.

Momlandia is a sobering place. Motherhood builds us up and breaks us down, flipping our brains on their sides and turning our hearts inside out. It exposes us. It's a mirror to all we hope to be, and all we are afraid to become. Add postpartum to the mix and you shoulder an unspoken haunt, a secret so many women carry in their pockets. It's just not one I'm willing to bear anymore. I must let the doctor's advice be good enough, and for now, I rest.

◆◆◆◆◆

JULY 10

I . . . CAN . . . SLEEP!

Hallelujah!

It's miraculous. I should have been using this progesterone from day one. And while I HATE the thought of medicine, the doctor says it's temporary.

You are so brave for following through.

I just don't like how shameful this feels. Here I was worried about my daughter toting a pacifier to the baby group. Wait until I take out my medication there.

You are fighting for your health. You just need a little help downregulating your nervous system right now.

Yes, I need my brain to shut off at night. Once my body remembers how to rest, she will wean me off.

Your body will remember soon. And look, you get to wean again!

Glory! It was super helpful talking to her, though. Women's health is still a black box. She said it's quite difficult to distinguish sleep deprivation from biochemistry, as they both have similar results.

Psychosis.

Yup. She said the hormone flux mothers experience is equivalent or WORSE than full-on menopause.

So now we are not only geriatric moms, we are also menopausal moms . . . without the perks of skipping our cycles?

Pretty much.

I'm so glad to be going through the Golden Girls era with you in my thirties.

◆◆◆◆◆

JULY 22

Mani-pedis in NY? My treat!

Oh, that sounds lovely. I actually just left the spa!

No way . . .

Well, I actually just left the dentist. But I got an hour to myself to put my feet up, and there was elevator music in the background.

Damn girl, you went to the spa!

What does it say about our lives that fluoride treatments feel like deep tissue massages?

That our husbands should fund an actual spa day for us.

So now that I'm two weeks into sleeping, my new theory for my daughter's insomnia is teeth.

Definitely teeth.

We invent these theories to feel better about their lives, don't we?

We need something to blame.

Today it's teeth. She's been growing them her whole life, apparently.

Should we be taking them to the dentist?

Do her three teeth really need a cleaning?

That question makes me feel better about my lack of awareness on this topic.

Just saying.

So, since you aren't nursing, what do you do to comfort her?

I'm giving her chamomile drops. And lots of holding.

I've heard clove oil is good too. You just rub a little on their gums.

I have cloves. I bought them to make hot-toddies at Christmas. Just add some oil?

Or you could just give her the Whiskey straight.

That was the mothering advice two centuries ago.

Maybe we bring that back.

Matching mom and baby flasks.

Everybody wins. But yes, you can make your own clove oil with some spices. Or you can pay twenty bucks for a microscopic bottle marketed for babies.

Like everything else in my life.

◆◆◆◆◆

AUGUST 1

Speaking of teeth, have you tried giving her liver?

Is that a serious question? What does liver have to do with teeth?

It's easy for her little teeth to chew. I can send you a recipe if you want. We've been giving Enora a simple liver pâté.

Pâté is not for me.

What are you cooking for her?

What am I cooking anyone? I don't think she can chew yet.

That's what I thought, but I'm now on this baby-led weaning kick. You give them long strips of food to hold, like carrot sticks, and they gnaw on it.

Won't they choke?

Oh, there are whole videos on how to distinguish a choke from a chew.

I don't think I can watch her hack on her food. I have enough to worry about. Purees for the win.

Whatever keeps us lucid is my motto.

Wait, are we still lucid?

♦♦♦♦♦

AUGUST 4

So, my new HR manager just explained to me that I should not expect the highest possible score on my annual review because I was away on maternity leave.

WTF.

She then quickly apologized and said that's not what she meant to say.

That's illegal.

Yup. And she knew it. That's why she retracted right away. And I work at an Ivy League University! This is the progress of women's rights.

I was going to ask for a raise this year, but I was on maternity leave during my contract talk, so I never had a contract talk.

These are the subtle ways that women's careers get put on hold, or even worse, regress, even if you keep working.

I mean, in order to even take maternity leave, you have to financially plan for life on a fraction of your salary.

While adding all the baby expenses. Meanwhile, I always thought if I didn't quit work, the career would keep rolling along as expected.

Do you know Scandinavia gives parents up to two years paid maternity leave? Even the dads are encouraged to take leave.

While Americans get twelve weeks at fifty-five percent.

Now there's a way to raise noble citizens.

And that's if you're lucky enough to have an employer with a parental leave plan.

Maybe I could submit a letter of recommendation for your annual review?

Oh, I'm taking a picture of my star chart and submitting it as evidence of my successful performance.

◆◆◆◆◆

AUGUST 7

Do you ever have nanny envy?

Like, do I ever want to BE my nanny?

Kind of. Some days, I'm convinced my child loves my nanny more than me. And frankly, she'd be smart to! My nanny is a real-life Mary Poppins with bags of baby tricks. It's truly her gift.

I think some people are just born to hang with babies.

I'm not sure I am one of those people. I love my baby, but I also enjoy my job (mostly). Does that make me a horrible mother?

It makes you a working mother, which feels like a lose-lose most days. When I'm at work, I feel like I should be at home, and when I'm home, I feel like I should be at work.

When I'm at home, I get bored sitting on the ground playing rattle for hours. I should enjoy rattle, right?

Some people are more skilled in the baby realm. You hang out with middle school kids at work. Most people run in terror from that age.

I can't wait until Isa is in middle school. I've got skills there.

She will reject all your skills by the teenage years.

Very true. It's just amazing the difference between how Isa acts with her nanny and with me. Isa lets her change her diaper. She eats all kinds of foods with the nanny. Life is sweet there, and by the time she gets home, all hell breaks loose.

Kids are always the worst behaved for their own parents. They feel the safest with Mom and save all the juicy emotions for us.

How endearing.

I try to reframe the daycare dilemma as Enora gets exposed to multiple roles of women throughout her day.

Yes, my therapist says that Isa is learning that women have many differ-
ent options in life. She sees her mom work, and that is a gift I'm giving to her.
My mom stayed at home with me, which was a different gift to me.

I think it's challenging to parent in a different way than our moms, because no matter what, we are fighting this internal blueprint. For example, your blueprint of a mom means stay-at-home mom, as that's who your mom was to you.

Exactly. My mother's main parenting goal was to prevent me from be-
coming a teen parent like she was. She scared all my boyfriends away until I
hit thirty; she was on a rampage for my education and career. Then, she did
a hard u-turn for a decade and wondered why I wasn't married or pregnant.
Now, she stares at me wondering why I don't stay home with Isa.

No matter what, we can't win. We need working mom mentors.

Our husbands can model skills too.

Yes, she will learn how to leave all her towels on the floor quite early in life.

Remember, we are trying to view the husbands positively?

Honestly, if she gets half the brains of Mateo, I won't need to walk her past MIT for the osmosis experiment. She will write her own ticket.

You do have a genius husband.

I do. Keep reminding me of that. We are blessed with exceptional men.

I'm glad my mom chased all my other boyfriends away. Even when I'm
mad at Jeff, he's still solid gold. Now if I could only get him to pack that diaper
bag.

♦♦♦♦♦

As a woman, I've been blessed to have a circle of ambitious friends—
women who are doctors, lawyers, educators, and directors. My generation of
women was raised by equally smart women, but our mothers did not have the
career options before us. My mother was pregnant at nineteen. Her dreams of
college got placed on hold until her sixth decade in life. Now in her seventies,
she's still working on her Associate's degree, and she's still the sharpest lady I
know.

My generation is the culmination of our mothers' unspoken dreams. We
were raised to follow our passions, pursue our goals, and fight for our imagin-
ings. Our mothers wanted nothing more than to grow us large wings. They
wanted their daughters to soar in their power and have AMBITION.

We got graduate degrees and climbed ladders. We knocked on closed
doors and demanded equal rights. We didn't settle for our partners, and we

established our careers before starting families. And then, at some point, we also wanted children. Could we now become ambitious mothers? Could children fit into those glass houses we were raised to break through?

In my experience, personal ambition and motherhood are in a stand-off duel, and neither lady wants to shoot first. As good women do, we were taught to get along and be polite. Better yet, let's pretend the duel isn't even happening by ignoring the tension altogether. Ambition? Motherhood? No tension there! Whatever you do, just don't start arguments.

But the duel runs deeper than ambition and motherhood. It revolves around the concept of SELF. We've placed motherhood in the SELFLESS camp, shrouding her with images of unattainable ideals. She is the saint who suppresses all personal interests (and feelings) to care of her child. She puts herself last. She is the good mom, holiday joymaker, the emblem of nurturing and sacrifice. She is the TRUE MOTHER (Theresa), martyr to the cause, and she will be praised.

Then we frame ambition on the SELFISH side, a word that screams bad, dare I say sinful or unfeminine. Ambitious moms are self-centered moms. If they still wanted careers, then why did they have children? Why are they still only thinking of themselves? Moms who won't martyr themselves for their children are second class mothers.

We need to untangle this. Quickly. Before one more mom or child gets squashed in the making.

Ambition isn't selfish. Self-care isn't selfish. It's part of being self-aware of what you need to then go care for others. For some, that's alone time. For others, it's creative work. For many, it's a workout. We all have different ways we recharge so we can then be present for others, for our partners, and for our children. This is how we lived pre-baby, and the same rules apply post-birth. Personal goals aren't self-serving. Having careers, hobbies, and goals that fulfill you create a HEALTHIER you—which you then take back to your family.

And further, we are told to practice self-care until we become a mom. Eat right. Exercise. Take alone time. Schedule date nights. And then, once we become mothers, at the very moment women MOST need self-care, we conflate self-care with selfishness. You want to exercise? But what about your baby?

Talk about backwards! Why on earth, in the biggest transition of a woman's life, the time she most needs to take care of herself (so she doesn't project her own issues onto her kid), do we suddenly tell her everything that previously made her whole is OVER! And do you know who tells her this the most? Other women and moms. The very people who need the same self-care!

Women, NO MORE! We are better than this. There's no need to become guilt-throwing lemmings that all jump off the cliff together. "Well, if I didn't get time for myself, you shouldn't either," we think. Great, let's all go drown together. Then there will be NO present moms to care for our children.

It doesn't make sense. When life gets stressful, you carve out MORE personal time, not less. You need more meditation, more healthy foods, more sweat, more calm. As my pastor used to say, "When your plate is so full you have no time to pray, clear out the first hour of your day to only pray."

We need some help, people!

When we make self-care and ambition selfish, everybody loses. We are worse moms. Our families get the worst of us. And we become unfulfilled people who mistakenly resent our families for our dissatisfaction.

Self-care's end goal is OTHERS. We take care of ourselves, so we have a self to offer others. We pursue careers that make the world a better place. That's the opposite of selfishishness, which seeks only personal gain. Trust me, when moms are on that rare date night, do you know who they are talking about? Their babies. There's no disregard of others happening. EVER.

We just have so few mentors to remind us that it's not selfish to have that date night. To the contrary, we are investing in a solid marriage from which to ground ourselves and our babies. Our kids need a healthy and balanced relationship modeled for them. It's helpful for them to see their parents like each other. Or their parents taking care of themselves. Or their parents as ALIVE. But it's hard to walk the tight rope act of mothering, partnering, self care, and work, particularly when we haven't often seen it done.

Strangely, the working mom is not new. In the ancient world, mothers worked all the time—they farmed the fields with the babies strapped to their backs. They were working, exercising, and getting girl time all at the same time. In rural parts of the globe, mothers still labor like this. But for most modern women, work and motherhood are compartmentalized into separate geographies. We "work" at the office. We "mother" at home. And our work is so removed from mothering, it's challenging to juggle both.

*We don't get very many "strap your baby on your back" office days. *(Oh just wait, we will in COVID 2020, which creates colossal amounts of unattainable mom standards.)*

And then you have motherhood itself—which alone is the hardest "work" I've ever done. So frankly, the whole dichotomy is complete BS. Stay-at-home moms ARE working moms. Working moms think about their kids ALL DAY LONG at work. Neither happens in a vacuum.

Nor does mothering. Ancient mothers never mothered alone. They mothered with others—aunts, sisters, grandmas, cousins. They collected gurus. There were twelve different hands available to hold their babies. Infant sharing was common. A baby got nursed by a herd of lactating mothers throughout the day. The infant had the joy of continuous contact, but not necessarily continuous contact with one woman.

Mothering has often been a GROUP project. Children are innately designed to make others around them fall in love with them, just in case something happens to their parents. There is a reason why people flock to babies; babies are flirts. And they've needed to be flirts to ensure their survival for centuries, as parents didn't always live to see their children grow. Even today in tribes where traditional ways of life continue, shared care is the rule, not the exception.

But you, modern mother, make sure you can juggle it alone, all by yourself, without batting an eye or making a complaint, you selfless, Mother Mary. And don't you dare be weak. Be feminine, loving, over-exerting, selfless, and a true Betty Crocker badass, but never ever weak.

Lies, all LIES.

We were not designed to solo mother, but few people admit this. Instead, we birth a baby and get handed a dictionary, where Mother has one definition: a superwoman who manages a household, a shiny baby, a marriage, and a social media feed of organic muffins—all while donning the latest yoga pants and mom trends. Then, if you are among the seventy percent of moms who work, you get passed the dictionary again. Definition: a Working Mom cares less for her child and more for herself. And by the way, you should be able to do both, so give your child her best life while raking in the dough.

Feel overwhelmed? Try harder.

You can't raise a baby on your own? How incompetent.

You can't make your work deadlines? You should quit.

You don't love rattle games all day long? Why did you even have a baby?

You need a babysitter? Or your own mother? Aren't YOU the adult now?

Daycare? You want her raised by strangers?

Judgment. Judgment. Judgment.

It wasn't meant to be this way. Women are not meant to mother in isolation, nor are we meant to bury ourselves under unreachable expectations. We have to start forgiving ourselves, and we have to expand our view of motherhood.

There is NO ONE WAY to parent. And if your parenting looks different from my parenting, that doesn't make yours better or worse. And if my parenting looks different from how I was parented, that's fine too. I'm grateful my mom stayed home with me. I'm grateful I have a career and my daughter.

But boy, these roots run deep. Our family trees grip us deeper than the redwood forests.

Self-care is not a luxury. Help is not a luxury. Fathers are not luxuries. Co-parents are not luxuries. Partners are not luxuries. Grandmothers are

DEFINITELY not luxuries. They are all meant to be in the mix with us, even as we live in societies that tell us to outgrow our families, follow our own paths, and move thousands of miles away. I did this, and don't get me wrong, it can be liberating—but one day, you grow up, learn that you can't do it on your own, and you still need your mother.

This is integration.

And while I fight it to my core, I surrender. I need others. I need my mother. I need my mom tribe. I need neighbors and cousins and friends and family to tackle this parenthood project and that does not make me a burden or make me weak. It makes me stronger. I need working mom mentors to show me a different way of being. I need time with my daughter and time by myself and time as a family. I need my own feelings about motherhood, even when they feel different from yours and ESPECIALLY when I'm not proud of them, because suppression is death.

And ALL of that's okay.

As a wise Presidentially-hopeful woman reminds us, "It takes a village."

As my therapist reminds, "Every feeling is acceptable." So, let's drop the labels of good and bad once and for all.

We are all doing our best. Cut others slack and cut yourself some too. The more we adult, the more interdependent we become. Grab a hand and start villaging. And if you don't have a village, fight to build one with those around you. Interdependence doesn't make you a bad mom; it makes you a better mom. Empty cups can't pour out water, and it's not selfish to feel full.

Selah.

◆◆◆◆◆

AUGUST 11

We are almost in NY! I can't wait.

I'm so excited. I have my bag all packed—not a diaper in sight, although I will be bringing my Spectra.

Should we plan activities near our hotel so you can go back and pump?

Nope. I pump all places. Bathrooms. Gas stations. Shameless milker right here.

How does afternoon Village shopping sound, followed by dinner and then a live band at a rooftop event?

Itinerary of my dreams.

Here's my packing list: sundress, sunglasses, lipstick, nightie, wedge heels, and earrings. I'm just bringing a backpack.

Sounds like you have a hot date.

I do. And remember, when we arrive, we have to try to talk about things other than our babies, at least over dinner.

Absolutely. This is a retreat to refuel our inner woman.

Does she still exist?

We will find her.

♦ ♦ ♦ ♦ ♦

AUGUST 15

Holy shiznit. This hotel is beautiful. And they oversold all their rooms with two double beds, so they gave us two adjacent rooms at no extra cost.

I'm just a few blocks away.

Did you bring toothpaste? Just realized that wasn't on the list.

I got ya, babe.

♦ ♦ ♦ ♦ ♦

If you are ever feeling frumpy, New York will receive and revive you. The city of ambition herself, she's been beckoning dreamers from around the world for centuries. She's a master at energy; you can't leave her presence without renewed vigor and a dash of pizzazz.

Oh, New York, thank you.

I lived in Manhattan for most of my twenties, and I left her for California. California has its own share of glamour, but nothing can pull you out of a frump like NYC. Sam and I accepted every invitation New York extended—coffee at iron-wrought tables in Bryant Park, East Village window shopping for shoes too expensive to wear, and late-night strolls through Gramercy pubs where sing-alongs were necessary. We played dress up in Zara and bought nighties in Intimissimi and fed our souls with GIRL TIME.

You know what I learned? Girl time is also not an indulgence; it is fundamental for fullness. Even if I can only schedule it once a year, the revival is strong. Sure, it's hard to not lug my baby stuff with me, mentally or physically, but Sam and I prepped by spending extra time with our littles before our excursion.

And then, we scheduled a full day of feminine rehab.

Moms, find ways to fill up. It's the best gift you can give your daughters. Please remind me of this next time I'm frazzled . . . so basically, next week.

♦♦♦♦♦

AUGUST 17

That was the most magical twenty-four hours I've had in a very long time.

It gave me hope that life is still possible.

There's nothing more renewing than sisterhood. I feel resurrected.

Can we do this every year?

Oh, I already have it on my calendar.

I think these are the most romantic texts I've had all year.

Hey, girlfriends hold our hearts in worthy ways. Are you home yet?

The bus just pulled into a Burger King. I'm pumping in the bathroom.

Enora needs to know what a saint you are for doing this for her.

I'm okay doing this one saintly task. I actually miss her. What a concept. She'll get the best of me when I'm home.

♦♦♦♦♦

AUGUST 24

So, are you leaping?

Hell, yes. New York, take me back.

Which leap is Enora in?

I think this one is the "process leap." The babies are learning sequences of items—what comes first, next, etc. Then at night, they process their new processes.

And their process makes everything hell.

This one's bad. She's waking all night.

Remember, these aren't sleep regressions; they are sleep PROGRESSIONS.

Remember, we don't buy that sh*t anymore.

Like most parenting advice. We've learned our lesson.

Trust our guts. Not other's guts.

We should have compassion for their growing brains, right?

I'd have more if her growing brain chose sleep.

It's time for everyone in this house to sleep. It's good for her. And it's good for ME.

Take no apologies.

✦✦✦✦✦

Sleep training is a bit like expeditioning through Nepal. In front of you is the Everest boulder, Mount Get My Baby to Freaking Sleep, and you must summit for sanity. So, you go to the baby store and buy all the survival gear: the blackout shades for the window light and the sleep sack to tuck the babies in tight. The white noise to mimic the sounds of the womb and sheepskin slippers to tiptoe out of the tomb.

I mean, the nursery.

Welcome to the wilderness of sleep training, where every trek guide will hand you a different summiting map. Some trails are short and steep, promising a full-night's rest in three days. All you have to do is listen to your child scream for three straight days. While this route has a heavy vertical incline, it will get you there quickly. But it's controversial and difficult to weather, without any subtle switchbacks. You basically boulder straight up that hill and arrive without oxygen.

Then there's the camping out method, where you prep your baby with basic skills at Everest Base Camp. Then, you camp out together for a few weeks. The baby goes in her crib, while the parent pitches their tent in the nursery. Once the child falls asleep, the parent tiptoes out of the room and returns to their own adult tent, madly praying that their exit doesn't awaken their camping infant.

Another method is Ferber, where you check on your child at various time intervals. This involves stopwatches, compasses to navigate the crib checks in the dark, night-vision baby monitors, and a stealth heart, as your little one will likely cry in between the checks. This method doesn't involve tip-toeing, as you leave the room entirely between check-ins. It also happens at Base Camp.

Then there's Pick Up-Put Down. This is what we've opted with for months, and although the method is self-explanatory, I read a whole book on how to pick up and put down my child. And then I picked her up and put her down three hundred times a night, until she fell back asleep. It's the only daily exercise I've had all year, deep knee squatting over her crib. Squat—lay baby down. Bicep curl—pick that baby up. I'm still waiting to see the results in my biceps.

Once you get to Base Camp, there's no turning back until the child falls asleep on their own. You hang out there until they learn, which means I've been living at altitude all year long. I thought this was progress, but at our next wellness check, the pediatrician dashes my climbing dreams.

"Does she fall asleep on her own yet?"

"No, she's still developing that skill. We hold her until she falls asleep, but she wakes up every time we put her back down."

"Well, you can only call it sleep training if it actually trained her. It sounds like she's still practicing."

Yes, thank you. I wish she was the infant the books mention, when I tuck her in and she proverbially dances with her stuffed bunny into dreamland. She's too smart for those tactics. Instead, she chucks her rabbit at my face, glaring, "That's no real bunny, honey. Hold me."

I admit, a recovering insomniac is likely not the best sleep trainer. I'm still learning to self-soothe; how in the world should I expect my mini-me to do it? I also swore I'd never be a person to hire parenting help. That's just way too bougie; the hot chef would be the automatic first hire anyway, should my budget allow, rather than a coach on nocturnal musings. But alas, I surrender. I need HELP, and I own it. My spare time becomes full of Googled baby trainers and completing online questionnaires.

Baby's sleep history? Non-existent.

Baby's temperament? Expressive. Persistent. Opinionated. Everything you want in a woman. Everything that's hard to parent as a child.

There's also a comment box for what we've tried. I assemble my confession, where I admit all my deep sleep sins—all those dark mom props I'd used to cheat my little angel into sleep, such as reading her forty bedtime stories and rocking her comatose or hiding her in bed with me. We've army crawled out of her room, straight Vietnam style, and WD-40ed every hinge in the house to not wake her. We now eat by candlelight in complete whispers. We've sung her midnight songs through the walls, crawled in her crib with her, camped, co-slept, and cried.

And we've failed. Our child still wakes every hour ALL night long.

As I prep for our first conversation, I brace to be dishonorably discharged from motherhood. All my friends' babies sleep through the night, some of them since birth. I must be doing something wrong with my crap sleeping skills. I grab my husband's hand, ready for the blows.

"Wow, it looks like you really love your child," the sleep coach says. "You've tweaked everything to make her comfortable. She's lucky to have such attentive parents."

I try to keep eye contract while fighting back the tears. Okay, actually I bawl in her arms. I don't feel attentive; I feel desperate and unskilled, except when shoe shopping in NY. But she sees through that anyway, and it breaks me. I not only sign up for her course, I ask if she can call me weekly for the next twenty years, just to tell me I'm an okay mom.

She laughs. I let her know I'm serious. That sh*t is rare.

"You just need some minor tweaks," she says. "All of the groundwork is there." We double up our blackout shades to make the room Nepalese-cave dark. We bathe Isa each night, instead of only when she's dirty. We move her bedtime up an hour. The coach teaches us how to differentiate her cries, learning which are emergencies and which are self-soothing. (Note: The first night, they ALL sound like emergencies.)

And voila, just like that, in a few weeks she's sleeping. I don't know what mountain shaman voodoo she did, but it worked and I'll take it.

We've summited the mountain. The view is beyond comprehension—a full night's sleep ahead of us each night. I hear birds singing again. I can see beyond today. My husband and I open a special bottle of champagne—one we've been saving for years for a major celebration. Seeing the top of Everest seems about right.

◆◆◆◆◆

AUGUST 26

Isa's walking! And she's sleeping!

That's great news. Enora is walking too just this week!

It's brilliant.

Way better than crawling.

I agree. She finally stopped eating all the dirt off the floor.

Everyone has been saying, "Watch out when they start walking. Then it gets harder because you have to chase them!"

I don't buy that. Every day that Isa gets older, the easier it gets.

Until they hit toddlerhood.

And middle school.

And boyfriends.

I'm sure they will date only marriage-material men, never the bad boys. (Extended pause).

They will skip the bad boys if they have good girlfriends.

That, my dear, we can surely show them how to do without reading any blogs.

◆◆◆◆◆

AUGUST 30

I'm prepping for another girl's overnight, thanks to my amazing Mother babysitter. I can't tell you how excited I am.

Grandmas for the win! Girlfriends for the win.

Oh, we officially moved Mom in for good. Everybody wins!

That's my next goal too.

I will say, I'm lamenting bringing my breast pump again. I almost started crying when I had to pull out the parts.

Maybe it's time? If our babies get no-tear shampoo, maybe we need some no-tear parenting.

Maybe it's time.

Or you can just breastfeed her until college. I hear it improves SAT scores.

And curbs them from dating.

Win-win-win.

You are right. Time to start the wean.

♦♦♦♦♦

SEPTEMBER 2

Happy birthday, sweet Enora! You are a smart, beautiful force in this world, and I can't wait to meet you in person!

We did it! One year!

I was assembling photos last night for Isa's first birthday party. Yes, I actually PRINTED photos, and I can't believe all the little stages we've grown though.

They do grow up so fast. I hate that cliché, but it's true.

We grew up so fast! I got more wrinkles this last year than ever.

Smile lines, my dear.

Very true. When I went to print the photos, do you know I took 23,000 photos last year? I can't even pick any to delete!

We are full-fledged families.

Baby made three.

♦♦♦♦♦

SEPTEMBER 14

Happy birthday to you, bright-eyed Isa! What a gift you are to the world! Auntie Sami can't wait to spoil you and kiss those cheeks!

Thank you! Her birthday is next week.

Wait, what day is it?

Her birthday is on the 24th.

No, I meant what day is it today?

Tuesday.

Dammit.

I love the enthusiasm.

Pretend nothing happened.

You are the first to wish her happy birthday!

♦♦♦♦♦

I had no idea that my child turning one would take an event planner—there are invitations to send, party favors to hand-make, taco catering to coordinate, organic baby snacks to purchase, guest lists to create, guests' food sensitivities to curate, food allergies of babies to avoid, color themes to select, cake flowers to match, and streamers to tape to the high chair.

All for an Instagram party picture she won't remember.

While every fiber of my being wants to bow out of the birthday comparison party, I also know this is a huge milestone. Your child only turns one once, and you only cross the first year of motherhood once. Plus, by the time Isa's big day arrives, I'd attended a half dozen other baby gala events hosted, of course, by my lovely mom group. These women have become my fortress, and since their children's birthdays came first, I got the perk of previewing their party hosting.

On the flip side, the bar had been set. My September Saturdays were filled with Martha Stewart-approved galas, the likes of which I had no idea how to host. You see, Martha and I have never been friends, let alone soul sisters. She makes cakes from scratch; I'm more of a box mix gal. She hand-knits her own sweaters; I shop at the thrift store. If I had my druthers, I'd wrap up a cardboard box at my house, put a candle in a cupcake, and turn on some Lady Gaga. To me, that's a real event.

But as I imagined hosting a cardboard box party, I felt a little sad for my daughter. She deserves her baby friends around. Sure, I'm trying to graduate from the SHOULD dilemma and own my parenting style, but maybe I can find a happy medium. It's rather hard to be the only mom in the mom group who skips the first birthday party. I vow to stop momparing on smaller tasks, such as others' jeans size, and indulge in the party bliss . . . my style.

First off, I choose a park. It's woodsy, natural, and cheap. I then pair my daughter's birthday up with an all-star planner mom. Her son and Isa were born three days apart. For our party, she handles the bulk of the creative work, and I approve whatever genius she Pinterests my way. Together, our children become one. They sit in their highchairs under an oak tree. We surround them with clothespin lines full of baby photos, a paparazzi of family, and all their crawling companions. They taste their first spoonful of sugar via the dairy-free/ gluten-free/ agave-blend icing on their naked mini-cakes.

Meanwhile, all the moms toast with cheers and champagne. Sure, it's our children's birthdays, but it's also our BIRTH days, that wild day when we became mothers. Speaking of then . . .

♦♦♦♦♦

One year ago, I was the world's roundest bridesmaid. False eyelashes dawned my face and cascading curls framed my brow. I wore a maroon sarong—those bridesmaid dresses that wrap forty different ways around you—and framed my budding belly with bows.

I was thirty-nine weeks pregnant. Thankfully, the bride loved me enough to overlook my obesity and host me in her bridal parade. Even more gratefully, her autumn wedding was in a vineyard. Wine would flow and shoes could be flat.

I had one wedding prayer for the couple: God, please don't let my water break at the altar. I had no problem being a beachball-sized bridesmaid, but I had deep issues hitting ten centimeters at the ceremony, particularly since my husband was the officiant. For safekeeping, we parked a get-away car behind the altar. The bride also invited three ER docs to the reception, any of whom, she assured me, could deliver upon necessity.

The morning of the wedding, Isa started moving. She wanted out. Signs of pre-labor began, and I knew it was go time. But, because I'm not a party-wrecker (and because I also deeply wanted to attend the wedding), I sat down and had a stern talk with my baby girl, just like I did the first day she existed.

Nine months earlier, my husband and I were evacuated from our home. It was a trying time—our town was recovering from mudslides and wildfires and many were couchsurfing, including us. That particular week, we were staying with the bride and groom-to-be. They were one of many friends who adopted our semi-homeless selves over the next few months. Mudslides take awhile to sort; our entire town was police-taped and prohibited as search and rescue continued. *Many lost everything, and at the time, we didn't know if our home was still standing.*

Amidst this chaos, I was unexpectedly one day late. I didn't think much of it, distracting myself by looking at bridesmaid gowns. (P.S. Bridesmaid gowns are the BEST distraction when ignoring natural disasters, as it takes years to find a non-tragic bridesmaid gown.) Since I was funneling my angst into wedding shopping, I was also ignoring my late period. Plus, my husband and I weren't actively trying, but when my cycle never showed, I took a pregnancy test in the bride-to-be's bathroom.

Many mothers cry when they get a positive test. I counted nine months ahead on my fingers and declared my first ambition of motherhood. "Sweetheart, I love you, but we are going to this wedding together! This is my last chance at being a bridesmaid, so please honor your mother's request. Love, Mom."

As I've learned now, many mom goals evaporate, but my pre-mom instinct knew differently. Even though the wedding and my child's due date overlapped, surely I could attempt both. This was my carrot-on-a-stick dream, as our town slowly put its life back together. My husband and I spent our whole first trimester moving from friend's couch to friend's guestroom, wearing borrowed shirts and shoes. But at least there was something elegant to anticipate: a wedding! I'm a sucker for ceremonies and public professions of love. Total weeper, right here. That wedding (plus my growing baby bump) kept me going during months of chaos, and I wasn't going to miss either event.

The doctors told me otherwise—I could either birth my daughter OR be a bridesmaid. To that small binary fate, I declared, where's the THIRD option?

Motherhood cannot be an either/or. We must fight for BOTH/ANDS, Ladies.

The morning of the wedding, she wanted out, I wanted her out, but there was work to be done first. I sat Isa down for her second mother-daughter chat. "Child, I'm putting on my bridesmaid Depends, we are gonna get through this evening in style, and then you and I are gonna go party in the delivery room."

She heard me. We danced the night away—mom, dad, and baby. We didn't steal away any attention; baby girl stayed put the entire time. The reception finished by midnight, where we retired our dancing shoes and crawled into slumber.

Three hours later, I was in active labor and three hours after that, I was five centimeters en route to the hospital. By the next morning, still in my bridal updo and fake eyelashes, I had a sparkling daughter in my arms.

God, why did it take me so long to listen? My first lesson as a mom needs to be blared from speakers, shuffled on repeat. FIND THE THIRD OPTION. It always makes everyone more radiant together.

◆◆◆◆◆

SEPTEMBER 25

I just found this picture of us pregnant together at my baby shower.
Look at our belly bumps touching!
We had no idea, did we?
None. Look how innocent we were!
So idealistic and young.
We curled our hair!
We have lipstick on!
I have way less crow's feet.
I look well-slept!
We had no clue what was ahead.
None. Some days I think, "I'm embracing this all-natural, beachy mom look," and then I look in the mirror and see a sickly Victorian child who won't last the winter.
And yet, we lasted the winter!
And leaky breasts.
And geriatric body pains.
And army crawling out of the nursery.
And appreciating our evolving marriages.
And thousands of bottle washings.
And dozens of dry shampoo bottles.
Year one. A masterpiece of memories.
Couldn't have done it without you.
Let's get deep for a second. What would you tell your former self in this photo?
That there is no perfect mom. And STOP WORRYING about everything.
She wouldn't believe that then. She may have to learn the hard way.
True. Okay, I'd tell her that the girl in the photo still exists so don't forget her.
She DOES still exist. We just gotta give her some time to show up again.
What have you most learned?
Grace. And while we are all called "moms," no one has the same job description and that diversity should be celebrated.
Amen.
Did you ever do a baby book?
This IS my baby book. Does that count?

Of course, but only if she reads it.

Well, it may not timestamp her first crawl, but at least it's honest.

♦♦♦♦♦

Dear Child,

You are the love of my life. Love isn't always easy, but it survives all things, hopes all things, endures all things. You took this woman and grew her into a mama. You are my greatest evolution, discovering you and becoming a mother. I am stronger because of your strength. I am more inquisitive, seeing there is so much yet to learn. I am grateful that, of all the mamas, God chose me as yours.

I hope I can do you justice.

One day, perhaps we can read this together and laugh at my misgivings. You can tell me what you were saying all the times I didn't understand. You can remind me of all the times I misinterpreted. And we can keep growing together.

If I can leave you with anything, I pray you grow up unafraid of your power. May your generation of daughters stand free from shame. May you be protected from mirages of perfection and grow confident in your own integrity. You don't owe anyone anything, nor do you have to be anyone but you. May you drop the vicious cycle of comparison; just opt out and opt in to the beauty of YOU. Above all, I pray you learn the power of trustworthy girlfriends— they are a refuge in life. Listen to who makes sense and let the rest fall away, but find deep soul sisters. They held my hands into motherhood. They will be the champions of your secrets—the juicy, the imperfect, the ugly, and the miraculous.

I'm always ready to listen too.

Through it all, holding you was my own greatest homecoming. Welcome home, little one. You are always welcome in my arms, and you will always be radiant to me. I wouldn't change a thing. I pray you find strength in your own skin, and as your Mama, I'll keep finding strength in mine. The globe is before us, the options are plentiful, so never take no for an answer.

Love you all the way to God,
Mom

When your children arrive,
the best you can hope for
is that they break open everything about you.
Your mind floods with oxygen.
Your heart becomes a room with wide-open windows.

—AMY POEHLER, *YES PLEASE*

"It doesn't happen all at once," said the Skin Horse.

"You become. It takes a long time. That's why it doesn't happen often to people who break easily, or have sharp edges, or who have to be carefully kept. Generally, by the time you are Real, most of your hair has been loved off, and your eyes drop out and you get loose in the joints and very shabby. But these things don't matter at all, because once you are Real you can't be ugly, except to people who don't understand."

—MARGERY WILLIAMS, *THE VELVETEEN RABBIT*

About the Authors

Educator and licensed therapist, Jennifer Strube spent nearly four decades assisting other people's children before venturing to have her own. A self-proclaimed non-domestic goddess, she enjoys foreign excursions, climbing mountains, glamping with her beautiful husband, and many other outdoor enterprises that get banished in Momlandia. To cope, she drinks way too much coffee, particularly while writing this confession (her 4th book). She works at a private school in California.

Samantha Lemos is a full-time wife, full-time mother, and works full-time at Harvard Medical School. Whenever she is not chasing her independent toddler, she loves sailing, pre-COVID world travel, opera dates with her genius husband, and spending time in nature. She is from Seattle, Washington and now resides in Boston, Massachusetts.

Samantha and Jennifer met while studying Psychology at Wheaton College. Together, they schemed ways to lure studious boys and overturn the world. As sophomores, they broke into their university library and hosted an overnight soiree in the theology section, while filming their first screenplay "Femmes Fatales." Twenty years later, their goals remain the same.

www.ingramcontent.com/pod-product-compliance
Lightning Source LLC
Chambersburg PA
CBHW070836100426

42813CB00003B/635